Yes, You Can Hear GOD too!

By Joan Pearce

Channel of Love Ministries

Channel of Love Ministries, Intl.
Joan and Marty Pearce
P.O. Box 458
Red Bluff, CA 96080
Phone: (877) 852-6194
www.joanpearce.org

ISBN 978-1-4276-3284-5

Cover and artwork design by Pamela Thomas Mahaffey

Dedication Page

I would like first of all to thank my Lord and Savior Jesus Christ for saving my soul and writing my name in the Lamb's Book of Life.

I want to thank the Lord Almighty for leading me and guiding me to write this book according to His will. To God be the Glory forever! Amen.

Without the leading of the Holy Spirit, this book would not have come about. For it is written, "'Not by might nor by power, but by My Spirit,' says the Lord of hosts." (Zechariah 4:6)

A personal thanks to my beloved husband Marty, and to my children: Alan, Rob and Carrie, for their encouragement to me.

I want to thank God for bringing me His servants who worked so many hours on this book. I thank God for the gift of wisdom He placed in them. I pray this book will inspire you who read it and bring you into a place of fulfillment and be an answer to your prayers.

A very special thanks to Pat McLaughlin for her countless hours of editing, and to Pamela Thomas Mahaffey for her hours of creative work on the design of the book and its cover.

There are so many others God has brought to me to be a blessing. There isn't enough paper in this book to thank them all by name. A sincere thanks to each and every one of you.

May God richly bless you!

Joan Pearce

1 On a Mandate from God 7
2 Hearing God — A Divine Appointment 13
• The Man on the Beach
3 It's Simple — Just Start! 19
• The Hitchhiker
4 The ABC's of Hearing God! 25
5 The ABC's Today 33
• The Bartender
• The Waitress and the Author
6 "For as many as are led by the Spirit...." 41
• Divine Protection
• The Drunken Man
7 Listen to the Holy Spirit 57
• We Are Your Help
8 Listening: A Personal Testimony 65
• Lord, my house?
9 Lifting Up Jesus 73
• Your Jesus
10 Soul Winner's Crown 83
• The Vision
11 Be A Light! 91
12 Life and Death Are in the Balance 95
• Gypsy Boy

13 On the Count of One! 105

• The Lady in the Brown Dress

14 A Compassionate Heart 115

• The Lady with the Bag of Groceries

• Men on the Freight Train

15 Street Rat 121

• Street Rat

16 Manifestations of the Holy Spirit 127

• What's So Funny?

17 The Anointing 137

• Expect A Miracle

18 Miracles Bring People to Jesus 141

• Issue of Blood

19 God Does the Miraculous......................... 147

• Woman in a Wheelchair

20 You are Chosen and Anointed................... 151

• The Twister

21 God's Perfect Timing 161

• The Lady at the Airport

22 God Will Make a Way 171

• Released from Jail

23 We Can Do the Will of the Father 177

• Ten O'Clock Meeting

Chapter 1

On a Mandate from God

While in deep prayer to God one day, God spoke to me about the End Time revival that will spread throughout the land, the great outpouring of His Holy Spirit. God gave me a mandate: "Tell and teach my people how to hear my voice. Their lives and the lives of their family members depend on them hearing Me.

"Tell and equip My church to hear Me. My End Time harvest of souls will come through an army of believers who know how to recognize My voice and obey."

The Lord gives voice before His army,
For His camp is very great;
For strong is the One who executes His word.
For the day of the Lord is great and very terrible;
Who can endure it?
"Now therefore," says the Lord,
"Turn to Me with all your heart,
With fasting, with weeping, and
with mourning."
So rend your heart, and not your garments;
Return to the Lord your God,
For He is gracious and merciful,
Slow to anger, and of great kindness;
And He relents from doing harm.

(Joel 2:11-13)

God wants all His body to know and recognize His voice and walk in the fullness of their destiny. As believers learn to clearly hear His desires, and His destiny for their lives the Holy Spirit will both lead and teach them.

Many in the church are crying out, desperate to hear from God.

"What do you have for me to do!"

"Where do I fit in Your over all plan?"

The End Time harvest of souls will come in as each of us fulfills the exact role God has for us. God has a purpose and a plan for each person.

When the Holy Spirit fell on the day of Pentecost, those who would bring forth the early church were together, in one accord.

> **And suddenly there came a sound from heaven, as of a rushing mighty wind, and it filled the whole house where they were sitting. Then there appeared to them divided tongues, as of fire, and one sat upon each of them.** (Acts 2:2-3)

The power of the Holy Spirit quickly mobilized the church. Peter, under the powerful anointing of the Holy Spirit, preached one message, **JESUS**, and three thousand were saved. Shortly after that, Peter and John preached to a lame man at the Gate Beautiful.

> **"Silver and gold I do not have, but what I do have I give you: In the name of Jesus Christ of Nazareth, rise up and walk."**
> (Acts 3:6)

Immediately five thousand more were saved. And so it continued.

The End Time harvest of souls will also happen quickly. It is critical that we be taught to recognize God's voice. As we hear and obey, the Holy Spirit will direct and lead us to people. Through the supernatural operations and manifestations of the Holy Spirit, we will see multitudes come to Jesus.

> **"...Not by might nor by power, but by My Spirit," says the Lord of hosts.** (Zechariah 4:6)

As happened in the early church, End Time leadership will come into position in order to disciple and care for this great harvest. The Holy Spirit will bring the leaders into position. Every gift will come into fulfillment by the Holy Spirit.

By hearing the voice of God, leadership in the body of Christ will be able to see and release the giftings in each congregation. Then God's army will arise and be released full strength, with everyone walking in their proper positions. This is essential, in order to undergird the last great final ingathering of the greatest harvest of souls, called the Latter Rain.

Be glad then, you children of Zion,
And rejoice in the Lord your God;
For He has given you the former rain faithfully,
And He will cause the rain to come down for you --
The former rain,
And the latter rain in the first month.
The threshing floors shall be full of wheat,
And the vats shall overflow with new wine
and oil. (Joel 2:23-24)

In verse 24, the threshing floor full of wheat is God's great harvest that is coming into His Kingdom. The vat filled with new wine and oil is the increase of God's great anointing called the Latter Rain. The miraculous power of God will flow through you, and through every other member of God's glorious church.

As all walk in their fullness, full of God's presence, anointing and love, cities and nations will see God's glory.

Alongside this great outpouring there will be also stress and persecution to the church. As we know His voice, God will divinely protect us from all danger. When we hear God clearly, He will show us who to talk to, where to go, whom to trust, where to meet, and how to pray. The manifestations of the Holy Spirit will be flowing through us. God will have a glorious church, without spot or wrinkle as we yield our lives totally to the operations of the Holy Spirit and hearing God.

I have been given a mandate from God to tell and teach the body of Christ to hear Him. *Yes, You can hear GOD too!* was written to prepare you for what is coming upon the earth. As you read this book, what is in the heart of God may rise up in you also. You may hear a cry come forth from deep down inside, "Oh I must hear You, God!" Perhaps the cry will continue until you even scream out from the depths of your heart and become overtaken with one desire: **"Oh God, I must hear You!"**

> **...the people who know their God shall be strong, and carry out great exploits.**
> (Daniel 11:32)

May this book help you learn to hear and obey God. It is just this simple: Hear God and Obey Him!

Chapter 2

Hearing God—
A Divine Appointment

Simple Christian principles such as, "Hear God and obey Him," are not always easy to put into practice. All Christians come to Jesus from the world, where they are used to hearing from the world. We are used to listening to and doing what our parent, friend, boss, teacher, or even ourselves thinks. We are used to choosing who or what we will even hear. How many of us have had a habit of ignoring someone who's telling us to do something, especially if it's something that is unappealing or seems inconvenient?

Nonetheless, hearing God and obeying Him really is simple. Consider what happens in the Military. New recruits are immediately put into training in a boot camp. One of their main objectives is to be sure everyone will hear the person in authority and immediately obey him or her. A new recruit must decide to hear and obey in order to remain in the military.

When we learn to be a hundred percent obedient to the leading of the Holy Spirit when God speaks to us about anything new, then we will have encounters with God. Let me share an amazing encounter with God, which happened to me.

The Man on the Beach

Many years ago I was in California doing a "God is Taking the City Program" with several churches. We had just completed a twenty-four hour prayer meeting at one of the churches. I was tired, and one of the women asked me if I'd like to sleep at her home instead of returning to where I was staying. I clearly heard the Holy Spirit say, "Go home to your apartment!"

When I got home, I dropped into bed and was instantly asleep. However after a very short nap, I sat up in bed and heard God say, "Go into Santa Cruz."

Santa Cruz was a forty-five minute drive away from where I was. I quickly obeyed! I arrived at a boardwalk and amusement park area where there were rides and games.

I asked God, "Do you want me to go to the Boardwalk?" He told me, "No. Go to the beach and sit by the lifeguard station."

As I sat there waiting to see what God wanted me to do next, I began praying, "God, is that the one? Or how about the person over there?" The Holy Spirit said, "Be still and I will speak to you."

We must be still and wait so that we will be able to hear God's still small voice when He speaks to us.

In the distance, I saw a young Hispanic boy who looked to be about eighteen or nineteen years old. He was walking on the beach, kicking sand. I heard the Holy Spirit say, "He's the one I want you to talk to." I started walking toward him.

When I got to where he was, I reached out and stopped him. He looked up at me and I said, "God speaks to me, and I believe He has something for me to say to you. Do you want to hear it?"

He looked at me as if I was a fruitcake! His body language was saying, "Leave me alone!" I asked him again, "Do you want to hear what God has to say to you?" He said, "Lady, I have the feeling I'm going to hear this anyway, so go ahead."

So I told him, "One month ago, you lost your girlfriend. She broke up with you. Then two weeks ago, you lost your job. And then you tried to commit suicide."

He looked up at me in amazement and said, "Yes...and in that exact order. How did you know?"

I said, "I told you God speaks to me! God wants me to say something else to you. Do you want to hear it?"

When he said yes, I went on to tell him, "God has a perfect wife for you and a perfect job. Suicide is not the answer to your problem. Jesus is the answer and He is all you need."

When I heard the Holy Spirit say, "Don't say any more. Go and sit down." I went back to my blanket on the sand, sat down and prayed, "Holy Spirit, save Him!" I was deep in prayer and travail for his soul.

The Holy Spirit said, "Look!" I looked down the

beach and the young man was on his knees crying! I said to God, "Holy Spirit, if you need any help, here I am! Bring him to my blanket."

For about forty-five minutes he walked the beach. He got within ten feet of me and I heard the Holy Spirit say, "Go to him and speak to him." I went over and asked, "Do you remember me?"

He said, "Yes." When God speaks to me concerning someone it's because that person has been crying out to God. So I asked him, "Have you been calling out to God?" He told me he had been out partying the night before and had gotten home very late. That morning at 8:45 (the exact time the Holy Spirit awakened me from my nap) a thought came to him to go to Santa Cruz.

Two weeks earlier, when he tried to commit suicide, he had had to attend a suicide clinic for counseling. While nervously waiting for his appointment, he read all the plaques on the office walls. One of them he read was about footprints on the beach. It told about a man during a time of trouble who went walking on a beach. As that man walked he realized there was only one set of footprints in the sand because Jesus was carrying him.

The young man explained that he was somehow led to go and walk on the beach at Santa Cruz that morning. He had the thought that God would come to him and pick him up out of all his sorrow and hurt.

"Is that what you really want?" I asked him, "for

Jesus to lift you up and heal you?" "Yes," he exclaimed; "Yes!"

I told him the plan of salvation, about Jesus' great love and awesome sacrifice. I said, "Right now, here on this beach, we can kneel and you can receive Jesus into your heart." We knelt and prayed, and he received Jesus as his Lord and Savior.

At 8:45 a.m. that day, the Holy Spirit awakened two people who lived in San Jose, California and spoke to them. By 9:00 a.m. we were both on our way over the same mountain pass to the beach in Santa Cruz, where there were three or four hundred other people. We were on our way to connect with God's miracle!

Several years later, I received a phone call from the young man I'd met. He told me he was now a youth pastor, and was dating a wonderful young lady!

Hearing God's Voice and acting on His direction meant new life for one soul, who would in turn go on to impact other lives for God.

You can hear God, too! It's simple. You can decide right now that you want to hear God and obey Him.

Oh what a wonderful experience it is when we learn to hear God and obey the leading of the Holy Spirit.

Chapter 3

It's Simple — Just Start!

When I first became a Christian, I was a baby in all Christian areas. I didn't know how to clearly hear the voice of God. Most new Christians don't know how to recognize God's voice. Just like a baby in the natural must be taught and nurtured, so we as Christians require teaching and nurturing. When we receive Jesus into our hearts, we begin the process of growing up in the things of the Spirit.

About three or four months after I was saved, I noticed that God was starting to reveal things to me. As I was listening to New Testament tapes, I noticed in the book of Acts, how those in the early church did everything by the Holy Spirit. God led his people by His Spirit to different areas, and to people's homes.

I found myself saying, "Lord, if the Holy Spirit worked through the early Church like that, why can't He work like that now? Why can't He work through me and through others in the same way?" I didn't have a lot of knowledge, so I began asking God questions. I had simply heard about something through my Bible reading and wanted to hear more from God about it.

When I was saved I had a business that required that I drive to different parts of Washington State. One day I was on my way to a sales training rally in Yakima, about a hundred miles from my home. As I drove, I was praying in the Holy Spirit. I remember praying, "Lord, tomorrow morning I want to be used by Your Spirit."

The next day I got up an hour early, to spend more time in prayer. I told the Holy Spirit, "Okay, I'm going to let You use me today. I'm going down to the restaurant and you can use me there between 7:00 a.m. and 8:00 a.m. But at 8:00 o'clock I have to head home, because I have an appointment."

I went to the restaurant at 7:00 a.m. and sat there having a cup of coffee. I sat quietly for an hour, asking the Holy Spirit who He wanted me to talk to or witness to.

As I looked around, I noticed there was no one in the restaurant except the waitress. Figuring she had to be the one, when she stopped to refill my coffee cup I told her I wanted to talk to her about Jesus. She smiled and said, "Oh, I already know all about Jesus! He's my Lord and Savior!" She briefly shared how she came to know Jesus and how much she loved Him.

When she left, I said, "Lord, there's no one else here. Who am I going to witness to? You've got forty-five more minutes left to use me!" As the minutes ticked away, no one entered the restaurant. That was strange, because the place was usually packed at that hour. When it was nearing 8:00 a.m., I thought perhaps I was to talk to the waitress about the Holy Spirit. She said, "Oh, I already have the Baptism of the Holy Spirit." As she walked back behind the counter, I sat wondering what was happening.

Feeling bewildered, I said, "I'm trying so hard to be

used by You, Holy Spirit. But I don't know how this works! Here I am just messing up this restaurant. They're not getting any customers because I'm here. I'm hurting their business. I'd better leave."

I paid the bill and went to my car. By then I was crying out to the Lord. It just seemed to be so hard to be used by Him. "Lord," I explained, "You had from 7:00 a.m. to 8:00 a.m. to use me and nothing happened. I guess I don't know how to hear Your voice." I laid my head on the steering wheel and started sobbing.

Suddenly I heard the voice of the Lord. "You don't have this right, Joan. I will use you when, where, and how I want to. You cannot tell Me at what time, or where I can use you."

I quickly got His message. "Oh Lord," I said, "is that how it works? You mean You want me to be on call all the time. That way, when You speak to me I will hear You and do what You tell me, the way You tell me to do it. Right?"

The Holy Spirit said, "Yes. Do you understand now, Joan?"

I said, "Yes. I do. That's so wonderful and awesome! I'm going to do that from now on." It's just that simple.

The Hitchhiker

I started the car and headed towards home. Suddenly, I came upon a man standing by the side of the road. He was just standing there. He didn't have his thumb out as if he were hitching a ride. It was the dead of winter and snowing. The man didn't have any luggage with him.

As I drove by him I heard a little voice inside of me say, “Pick him up.”

I thought, “I’m not going to pick up a total stranger! This must be the devil trying to trap me.”

I drove a little further and heard the same voice again. “Pick him up.” I responded with, “I rebuke you, Satan! I’m not picking up a stranger! I could get into trouble that way.”

Then I heard the voice say, “I thought you said you would obey Me.”

“Is that You, Holy Spirit?” I cried.

“Pick the man up,” He said.

I put the car in reverse and backed down to where he was standing. Then I leaned over, opened the door, and said, “Hey mister, do you want a ride?” He came over, looked inside, and said, “Lady, don’t you know better than to go picking up strangers on the road? You could get in trouble doing that.”

“That’s true,” I told him, “but the Holy Spirit, God Almighty, told me to pick you up. So, do you want a ride?” Notice here that I had several confirmations from God before I stopped and picked up a hitch-hiker.

When he jumped into the car, he seemed very happy and excited. He told me he’d been standing out in the cold for an hour, trying to catch a ride. He’d had his thumb out for awhile. Then he said, “You see, I just got out of Walla Walla State Penitentiary.”

Immediately I thought, "Oh my God, I picked up a man who just got out of prison, and this is my first time hearing the Holy Spirit!"

He went on to say that while in prison he had given his heart to Jesus and gotten saved. He was serving Jesus and attending Bible studies there. He'd just been released and needed a ride back to Sunnyside, Washington. He told me he had stayed all night in the coffee shop and didn't have any money left. He'd been out trying to get a ride, with no success.

He told me he'd given up trying, and told the Lord he was going to put the word into action. Then he had closed his eyes and told the Lord, "Father in heaven, You said You would "**supply all [my] needs according to [Your] riches in glory by Christ Jesus"** (Philippians 4:19.) I need a ride. So I'm just going to stand here. I'm not even going to put out my thumb. You said to **"ask, and it shall be given to you"** (Matthew 7:7), and I'm asking You, Father. I'm your child. I gave my heart toYou. So I'm going to wait here for a ride. Even if they find me buried frozen here in the snow, at least I trusted You for a ride."

He told me that as soon as he'd finished praying, I pulled up and told him God wanted me to pick him up.

"Praise God!" I was literally shouting. I was so excited I felt like jumping all over the place. I had heard from God!

I told the man how nervous I was about picking

him up and how I wondered if I was really hearing from God. But it was God!

The man turned to me and said, "I'm so glad you heard from God!" There we were, two brand new Christians, so excited because we had both heard from God.

I drove him all the way home. I got to meet his family and share Jesus with them. As we shared our recent experience of meeting on the road, I was able to tell them, "I know how to hear the voice of God!"

You also can hear the Voice of God!

Chapter 4

The ABC's of Hearing God

What if the Holy Spirit began speaking to you right in the middle of cooking dinner? Or what if you began to hear His voice while on your way to work? Would you listen to Him and obey what He told you? Or would you go on with your own plans and agenda?

Many times the Holy Spirit asks us to do something that is inconvenient. As children of God we desire to hear God. When we allow Jesus to be Lord of our lives that means that we are willing to do whatever He asks us to do. As children of God we are to be obedient to the voice of His Holy Spirit.

The apostles and evangelists of the early Church preached the Word of God everywhere they were sent. They were scattered to all parts of the world to preach the Word. In chapter 8 of Acts, we read about Philip, the evangelist.

> **Then Philip went down to the city of Samaria and preached Christ to them. And the multitudes with one accord heeded the things spoken by Philip, hearing and seeing the miracles which he did. For unclean spirits, crying with a loud voice, came out of many who were possessed; and many who were paralyzed and lame were healed. And there was great joy in that city.** (Acts 8:5-8)

Evangelists in ministry continue to experience things similar to what Philip experienced. When we do revival meetings in an area, after a week or so there is much joy in that city or town. By then many people have experienced salvation, healing and deliverance.

But notice what happened to Philip. While he was right in the midst of a great and very successful revival, the Holy Spirit suddenly told Him to leave and go somewhere else.

> **Now an angel of the Lord spoke to Philip, saying, "Arise and go toward the south along the road which goes down from Jerusalem to Gaza." This is desert.**
>
> **So he arose and went. And behold, a man of Ethiopia, a eunuch of great authority under Candace the queen of the Ethiopians, who had charge of all her treasury, and had come to Jerusalem to worship, was returning....** (Acts 8:26-28)

What happened to Philip illustrates some important things about how God works with those who are committed to seeking and doing His will.

Steps in Hearing and Obeying the Holy Spirit

A. Get into position.

Philip was instructed to go out into the desert. In understanding how to obey the Holy Spirit, we find the first step is getting into position. It's important to realize that many times God begins speaking to you by directing you to a location or place where the miracle is going to occur. You have to be in position.

Suppose Philip had told God, "I'm in the middle of a revival where I am. I don't want to go out into the desert. You can't be asking me to leave here now!"

You can respond like that, but if you do someone's life might be hanging in the balance. God may require you to stop what you are doing, even something you have been doing for Him, to get you to a particular place, just to have you ready.

To do anything for God, of course you have to hear what he wants you to do. But if you decide to wait until the Holy Spirit tells you His whole plan from beginning to end, then you will hinder the Spirit from being able to use you. God is waiting for you to be obedient to His first instructions before He'll give you any more. Will you simply go and get into proper position so that someone can get his or her miracle?

B. Wait in position for further instructions.

Once you get into position, God will reveal the next step to you. He will usually only show you a little bit at a time. In Philip's case God removed him from a successful revival meeting and had him go into the desert. Now Philip was in position for what God had in mind, so God could give him further instructions.

> **Then the Spirit said to Philip, "Go near and overtake this chariot."**
>
> **So Philip ran to him, and heard him reading the prophet Isaiah, and said, "Do you understand what you are reading?"**
>
> **And he said, "How can I, unless someone guides me?" And he asked Philip to come up and sit with him.** (Acts 8:29-31)

The Holy Spirit sent Philip, in answer to the questioning of someone who was studying the Scriptures.

C. Simply lift up Jesus, showing them Scriptures.
The Bible says:

> **How then shall they call on Him in whom they have not believed? And how shall they believe in Him whom they have not heard? And how shall they hear without a preacher? And how shall they preach unless they are sent?**
>
> **As it is written, *"How beautiful are the feet of those who preach the gospel of peace, who bring the glad tidings of good things!"***
>
> (Romans 10:14-15)

To see others come to a saving knowledge of Jesus Christ, all that's needed is to lift up Jesus. Preach the simple message of Jesus. How will people understand unless we simply show them what the Word of God says in the Bible, and explain who Jesus is to them?

The Holy Spirit can help us keep it simple: "Jesus, the Son of God, died on the cross. He paid the price for our sins. When you invite Jesus into your heart, you receive the gift of salvation." Souls are won through the simplicity of the Gospel.

The eunuch sitting in the chariot was reading Isaiah 53:32, **"He was led as a sheep to the slaughter; and as a lamb before its shearers is silent so he opened not his mouth."**

He asked Philip,

> **"Of whom does the prophet say this? Of himself or of some other man?" Then Philip opened his mouth, and beginning with this Scripture, preached Jesus to him."** (Acts 8:34-35)

It's evident that Philip gave a good explanation of the Word of God. The Ethiopian quickly understood that he needed to identify himself with the death, burial and resurrection of Jesus. Then he confessed with his mouth that he believed Jesus to be the Son of God.

> **Now as they went down the road, they came to some water. And the eunuch said, "See, here is water. What hinders me from being baptized?"**
>
> **Then Philip said, "If you believe with all your heart, you may." And he answered and said, "I**

believe that Jesus Christ is the Son of God."

So he commanded the chariot to stand still. And both Philip and the eunuch went down into the water, and he baptized him."

(Acts 8:36-38)

The Bible says:

...if you confess with your mouth the Lord Jesus and believe in your heart that God has raised Him from the dead, you will be saved. For with the heart one believes unto righteousness, and with the mouth confession is made unto salvation. (Romans10:9-10)

The eunuch did what the Scripture says. He believed in his heart, and confessed with his mouth. Then he desired water baptism, which is the outward expression of the inner cleansing of the soul through Christ. Philip had fully answered the eunuch's questions.

Now when they came up out of the water, the Spirit of the Lord caught Philip away, so that the eunuch saw him no more; and he went on his way rejoicing. (Acts 8:39)

Can you imagine how astonished this Ethiopian eunuch must have been? No sooner had he come up out of the water from being baptized, than he found that Philip had disappeared. They were in the desert, with no one else around them. Philip had been translated by the Holy Spirit to another city. His physical body was supernaturally transported through time and space to another location for another assignment!

The eunuch must have been in awe, and may well have thought that Philip was an angel. Even so, this brand new Christian went on his way rejoicing in God.

The Lord desires to reach out to his people. He knew this eunuch was in the desert, crying out to Him. God had to get Philip out into the desert so that there could be a miracle.

When you hear the Holy Spirit, be obedient! Remember your **ABC's**.

A. First, the Holy Spirit will get you into position.

B. Then the Holy Spirit will give you direction about what to speak and what to do.

C. Finally, through the simplicity of preaching the Gospel, and through your lifting up Jesus, someone will be saved, or a seed will be planted into their heart.

When you open your mouth to speak the Holy Spirit will put words in your mouth.

The same Holy Spirit who raised Jesus Christ from

the dead is operating in believers across the world today. God's will is to use you. His Holy Spirit will walk, talk and do miracles through you because God anoints you to do it!

God is willing and able to use you if you will let Him.

Jesus said, "If I be lifted up, I will draw all men unto Myself."

Chapter 5

The ABC's Today

It's important to know that the ABC's that are being discussed really work right now in today's world. The Holy Spirit desires to use you, just as He used Philip. The two stories in this chapter illustrate how the Holy Spirit is continuing to work through His people today, just as He did two thousand years ago.

The Bartender

A few years ago we were working in a church in Prunedale, California, a small rural community, where houses were scattered about in the countryside. At one of the services we grouped people in twos and threes and went out witnessing door to door, wherever the Holy Spirit would lead us. It is a truly amazing thing when you allow the Holy Spirit to lead you to where you should go.

As we were driving down the road, praying in the Spirit, the Holy Spirit literally told us to turn left, turn right, go this way, and go that way. We simply allowed the Holy Spirit to direct the car. Suddenly we had the impression to go over a hill. We came to a long driveway leading to a house, and the Holy Spirit impressed upon us to go there.

There were big dogs in the fenced front yard. They looked ferocious, so I suggested we drive to the back. We got out of the car and knocked on the back door. We were not dressed up like "Christians," in fancy dresses or business suits. Instead we had on casual, comfortable clothing. We carried pocket New Testaments, rather than large Bibles, so we wouldn't scare people away.

When we knocked, a man's voice said, "Come in." We didn't think a few strangers should just walk in, so we knocked again. Again the man called out, "The door's open, I said come in."

As we entered the kitchen area, we could see a living room at the other end of the house. A man popped his head out from one of the adjoining rooms and said he would be with us in a minute. He asked us if we wanted a beer. When we declined he began calling out the names of other alcoholic beverages. We declined again. When he offered sodas we accepted and just looked around the house as we waited.

On the dining room table we found a huge Bible opened to the Book of Revelation. Another Bible was opened to Matthew. He had all kinds of Bibles, even a cartoon one, as well as a *Strong's Concordance*. The whole table was covered with Bibles and Bible related materials. Everything looked new and unused.

I said to the others, "Look, he's been studying Revelation." About that time the man came into the room. He was carrying a huge tray and had a towel draped over his arm. He served us drinks with straws in them and had extra things on the tray like olives and lemon slices. I said, "Wow! You've got all these Bibles. Have you been studying?"

He said, "Lady, you won't believe this. You see, I'm a bartender. Every Friday night all my friends come down to the bar. After hours, when the bar is closed, I buy them booze and they stay until six in the morning. They all get drunk. Last night I told them I didn't want to do that anymore. At 2:00 a.m. I was going to close the bar and go home. Usually I'd spend $250.00 buying them all booze.

"This morning I don't know what got into me! I went downtown to the Bible bookstore and look what I bought!" He brought out another bag of books and Bibles, and showed us a $250.00 receipt.

He said, "This Bible is supposed to help me. That Bible dictionary is supposed to help me. I've been sitting here for hours, trying to figure things out. I started reading Revelation in this one, and Matthew in that one. I couldn't understand a word of it. Finally I just threw up my hands a few minutes ago. I told God that if He really wanted me to understand all this stuff He would have to bring help. I'd just gotten up to fix myself a drink when you knocked on the door. So what do you guys want? What are you selling?"

I said to him, "Well, we must be the answer to

your prayer. We're your help!" When he asked me to explain, I told him how God had directed us to his house. I told him, "Until you accept Jesus Christ as your Lord and Savior, you will never understand the Bible. Your understanding is blocked. This blockage is removed when someone invites Jesus into his or her heart. Once you receive Jesus into your heart, He will open up the Bible to you. All of a sudden everything you have been reading will begin to make sense to you."

"Really?" he asked. "Yes," I said. "We know because we're Christians." He said, "I've been trying to figure out how to be a Christian, but I don't have anyone to guide me."

Remember how the Ethiopian eunuch told Philip about not having anyone to explain to him what the Scriptures meant. This man in Prunedale, California was in a similar situation. He needed someone to guide him in the Scriptures. We shared the simplicity of Jesus, just as Philip did. We lifted up Jesus and the cross of Calvary. After about fifteen minutes of sharing the Word, the man who was a bartender asked Jesus to come into his heart and be his Lord and Savior.

That bartender had been soul-searching for God and he came to know Jesus. We, as the Church, need to truly understand that unless someone guides them, people will not know God. We are to guide others to the Truth! The word says, **"And you shall know the**

truth, and the truth shall set you free" (John 8:32.) The Word of God is the Truth everyone needs to hear.

As you follow the basic principles of listening to and obeying the Holy Spirit, you will learn to stop what you are doing, even at a moment's notice, and allow God to lead you in lifting up Jesus so that lives can be saved and changed forever! What happens is truly up to God and to the people you speak to.

The Waitress and the Author

I will always remember one day when I was at home, right in the middle of cleaning one of the bathrooms. I was almost done cleaning the whole house. Suddenly I heard the Holy Spirit say, "I want you to go to this specific restaurant, right now." I said, "But Lord, I'm almost done with all my housecleaning. I only have this bathroom left to clean!"

As I started wiping down the bathroom mirror, the Holy Spirit said, "Right now! Stop what you're doing!" I figured I'd better go!

I went into the restaurant and stood by the door waiting. As I've mentioned, you have to wait to hear directions from the Holy Spirit. I said, "Okay, Lord. Where do you want me to sit?" And He said, "See that seat over there? Go sit there." I went to the seat and sat down.

The Holy Spirit said, "Ask the man sitting beside you how he feels when people talk to him about Jesus in a public place. Tell him you're writing a book."

Actually I was writing a book, *Let's Go Fishing*, which is about soul winning. When I asked him, he said, "It's really strange you would ask me that question, Lady." "Why?" I asked.

He explained that just before I arrived, a woman sitting where I now sat had had an on-going conversation with the waitress about Jesus. He'd listened to all of it, and it hadn't bothered him at all.

Just as he was telling me this, the waitress approached to pour me some coffee. So I asked her, "How do you feel when people talk to you about Jesus in a public place?"

"I can't believe you're talking to me about Jesus!" she exclaimed. "Another lady who was just sitting there was talking to me about Jesus! The strange thing is that my boyfriend is a Baptist. He just told me he couldn't continue dating me unless I received Jesus and got born again." (The term "born again" refers to when you surrender your life to Jesus and have a personal relationship with Him.)

"We had an argument last night," she continued, "and he talked about Jesus until three in the morning. When I got to work that lady was telling me about Jesus. Now you're telling me about Him. I think God must want me to get saved! Three people in the last few hours have spoken to me about Jesus! How do I do it? How do I get saved?"

I made arrangements with her to be back at the

restaurant at the end of her shift. She gave her heart to Jesus, making Him Lord and Savior of her life.

God certainly knows how to get our attention! Because I stopped washing my bathroom mirror and obeyed God, two lives were changed forever. God knows how to get us to the right place at the right time so that a soul will get saved, if we will just hear the Holy Spirit and obey. It took several people speaking to that waitress about Jesus, but God knows what each of us needs.

The day after the waitress received Jesus, I was talking with my friend, Ann, who often went witnessing with me. As I told her what happened she became very excited. "You're not going to believe this," she said. "I'm the woman who was sitting in that seat in the restaurant yesterday morning, talking to that waitress about Jesus."

The Holy Spirit did even more! When I was in the restaurant, I had also questioned a man about his attitude towards people who spoke about Jesus in public. As I was leaving, I reached over and gave him a little book I wrote called *The Empty Spot*. It's a book that encourages people to reflect upon the part of each of us that needs Jesus. Over the years thousands of people have come to Jesus through reading this book.

Several months later, that man I'd given the book to called me. "I tried to throw your book away three times," he said, "but I kept having to retrieve it from the garbage. I don't know why I'm calling. I don't understand all this!"

I asked him if he'd read the book, and he said "No, but I can't throw it away."

As we talked he told me he just had a few weeks to live. He said, "I'm going to Europe to try to locate an old girl friend, and I plan to die there."

"You don't have to die," I told him, "Jesus can heal you and you can live. I can arrange to meet you and pray for you."

"I can't," he said, "I'm flying to Europe tomorrow morning." My response was, "Your life depends on this. You need to meet my friend and me and let us pray with you."

He rearranged his flight and met me and my friend Ann the next day. It was an all day ordeal, but at the end of it he was delivered from death, received Jesus as his Lord and Savior and was filled with the Holy Spirit.

I believe God has a wonderful sense of humor. He had me mention to that man that I was writing a book. The man turned out to be the author of several books. He's still an author, and is serving God today. God knows just how to help you reach others for Him.

Chapter 6

"For as many as are led by the Spirit..."

The same Holy Spirit who performed the miraculous during Jesus' time is the same Holy Spirit who does miracles today. Many people question how the Holy Spirit operates. Does the same Spirit work in both an adult and a two year old? Does the Holy Spirit work even through a young child? The answer is yes to both questions. When any person, adult or child, receives Jesus and then the Holy Spirit, they receive the same power that worked through Jesus! The Bible says:

> **"...how God anointed Jesus of Nazareth with the Holy Spirit and with power, who went about doing good and healing all who were oppressed by the devil, for God was with Him."**(Acts 10:38)

I have personally witnessed children as young as three or four years old operate in the power of the Holy Spirit.

Divine Protection

A missionary who had just returned from the Philippines attended one of our revival meetings. During the several years he and his wife had lived in the Philippines, they'd had several children. He came to me after one of the services and said, “Sister Joan, I have been worrying myself sick over my children ever since my family and I returned to America. Every time I see pictures of missing children on a milk carton here, I have visions of one of my teenagers or little ones being kidnapped on their way to school. Here in America there seems to be so much violence and crime. In the Philippines we lived in the bush where these kinds of things never happened around us.

I’ve been praying about all of this. The Holy Spirit told me that if my wife and children receive the baptism of the Holy Spirit and pray in the Spirit, He will lead and guide them. They will become sensitive to the leading of the Spirit and know how to avoid people and situations that might harm them.

The missionary invited me to his home to pray for his family to receive the baptism of the Holy Spirit. We had the family gather in a circle in the living room and led them in prayer. They began to speak in other tongues as the Spirit gave them utterance.

Suddenly their three-year old son began to prophesy! He prophesied over his brothers and sisters; he laid hands on his father and he spoke mighty words over his family.

It really is the same Holy Spirit at work, whether the person is an eighty-year old adult or the three-year old son of a missionary.

It is essential that God’s people learn to allow the

Holy Spirit of God to lead us in everything we think, do and say. The world is looking for miracles. People want to see the power of God. That's why they call psychic hotlines, and go to fortune-tellers and palm readers. They are really searching for what the Church of Jesus Christ should be giving them.

As believers in Christ, we are the anointed ones, because God has anointed us! God has told His people to go out in the authority, power and anointing of His Holy Spirit to lift up Jesus. The work of the Holy Spirit is to direct people to Jesus.

In John, chapter 5, the Scribes and Pharisees asked Jesus by what power and authority he did miracles.

> **Then Jesus answered and said to them, "Most assuredly, I say to you, the Son can do nothing of Himself, but what He sees the Father do; for whatever He does, the Son also does in like manner."**
> (John 5:19)

Jesus was explaining to them His total obedience to the Father in everything. He only does what the Father shows Him to do, and He only says what the Father tells Him to say. His obedience is absolute.

> **"...He humbled Himself and became obedient to the point of death, even the death of the cross."**
> (Philippians 2:8)

We who follow Jesus must learn to be totally obedient to the leading of the Holy Spirit just as He was.

> **"I can of Myself do nothing. As I hear, I judge; and My judgment is righteous, because I do not seek My own will but the will of the Father who sent Me."** (John 5:30)

It is astonishing to realize that Jesus, the Son of God, said He could "do nothing" of Himself, but only what He saw the Father doing. If it was that way for Jesus, who do we think we are to consider we could do anything without the help of the Holy Spirit? As we seek the will of the Father and the leading of His Holy Spirit, we will see people coming to Jesus, just as they did in the Bible.

In the book of Acts, we read that the Apostle Paul heeded the Holy Spirit's direction, which was given to him in a vision.

> **And a vision appeared to Paul in the night. A man of Macedonia stood and pleaded with him, saying, "Come over to Macedonia and help us."**
>
> **Now after he had seen the vision, immediately we sought to go to Macedonia, concluding that the Lord had called us to preach the gospel to them.**
>
> (Acts 16:9-10)

A vision from the Lord convinced Paul to change their traveling plans. He and Silas were obedient to the Holy

Spirit. They went not knowing what to expect, only that the man in the vision was asking for help.

It's so important in soul winning to always be ready to act as the Spirit leads. You cannot just stand there saying, "Well, I'm just going to wait for three dreams and a vision before I go out and tell someone about Jesus." No! We are all called to go into all the world and preach the Good News (the Gospel). Telling people about Jesus is something you need to do every day!

Paul and Silas went to Macedonia. While they waited for direction from the Holy Spirit about whom to speak to, they remained busy about the Father's business.

> **And on the Sabbath day we went out of the city to the riverside, where prayer was customarily made; and we sat down and spoke to the women who met there. Now a certain woman named Lydia heard us. She was a seller of purple from the city of Thyatira, who worshiped God. The Lord opened her heart to heed the things spoken by Paul.**
>
> (Acts 16:13-14)

The riverside was a trade center. Today, we might compare it to a shopping mall. As the two disciples spoke to a group of women there, apparently Lydia, who had set up her booth nearby to sell her purple cloth, overheard what they were saying.

From what happened with Lydia we can learn how important it is to talk about Jesus. You never know who may be listening in. When you're having a conversation in a restaurant, on a bus, or even in an elevator, others may also be hearing your words. It may well be that God will open the heart of that one who is just overhearing.

As Christians, we should be talking about Jesus wherever we go, when we're out to lunch, in a store, or doing any of our other daily activities. Though Lydia was just listening in on Paul's conversation with the other women, it was her heart that God opened. And God did even more than that!

> **And when she and her household were baptized, she begged us, saying, "If you have judged me to be faithful to the Lord, come to my house and stay." So she persuaded us.** (Acts 16:15)

Remember, Paul and Silas had arrived in Macedonia without having any place to stay. They had made plans to travel in a different direction. In Macedonia, they had gone to the riverside to be obedient and talk to people about Jesus. Then suddenly, not only were Lydia and her whole household saved when God opened their hearts to receive Jesus, but Lydia invited them to stay in her home.

Because they obeyed the leading of the Holy Spirit, these men were amply provided for, with lodging, food and clean clothing. God provided by working through a brand new convert. You needn't worry about your needs when you go out to preach Jesus to people. You can trust God to take care of everything.

Now it happened, as we went to prayer, that a certain slave girl possessed with a spirit of divination met us, who brought her masters much profit by fortune-telling.

This girl followed Paul and us, and cried out, saying, "These men are the servants of the Most High God, who proclaim to us the way of salvation." And this she did for many days.

But Paul, greatly annoyed, turned and said to the spirit, "I command you in the name of Jesus Christ to come out of her." And he came out that very hour. (Acts 16:16-18)

Notice that Paul spoke to the spirit, not to the slave girl. This slave girl spoke true words about Paul and Silas. She said they were proclaiming Jesus and sharing the way of salvation. However it is very likely she was speaking sarcastically. The spirit used her to say true words in a way that annoyed, ridiculed and criticized the men of God.

The Drunken Man

We had an experience that was similar to Paul's with the slave girl, while we were working on street evangelism with the youth group from a Seattle church. There was a long strip in their area that was a teenage hang out. Hundreds of teens regularly gathered on the streets and cruised by in their cars. As part of our training, we gathered their church group of seventy-five to a hundred teens and took them out on the streets. The young people were divided into groups and assigned team captains. Groups were then placed every four or five blocks along the strip.

We prepared sandwiches, drinks and snacks to be given out to the street people as we were talking to them and witnessing. I watched over the whole strip. If problems occurred they could come and get me. One of the team leaders came to me urgently, about a man who was harassing the teens in one of the groups. Though he was politely told to stop bothering the girls, this man just kept on doing it.

When I arrived at their location, I quickly saw that the man had been drinking. Yet it was clear that even though he was intoxicated, he knew the Word of God. As the teens were sharing the Scriptures with others, he started quoting some Scriptures word for word. He was choosing good Scriptures for evangelism too! However even though he appeared to be very knowledgeable about the Bible, he was clearly annoying the young people from our group who were there to evangelize, and he was distracting to their efforts.

I went up to him and said, "Sir, I can tell you know the Word of God. However this is the first time these youth are out witnessing and you're interrupting them. You're not letting them be led by the Holy Spirit. Besides, you're drinking and it doesn't look too good, and you're butting in. They really don't need your help in witnessing right now."

He looked at me and said, "I don't like you! Who put you in charge here anyway?" "Look," I told him, " I'm in charge of this youth group. I have the pastor's permission to have the youth out here. I don't want you bothering them anymore."

Though he said he would stop, and he actually walked away, half an hour later I was notified that he had moved down two blocks. Now he was bothering another group.

When I spoke to him again, he just looked at me and said, "I don't like you lady!"

This time, he had a beer bottle in his hand, and I could tell it was not him speaking to me. I was in a situation similar to Paul's when he was confronted by the slave girl. Paul had to command the spirit that was in the slave girl to leave. The problem wasn't with the girl herself. There was a spirit in her. I said to the drunken man, "In the name of Jesus Christ of Nazareth, I command this spirit to stop tormenting!"

Then he got really angry with me, saying, "I don't like you!" He started to throw his beer bottle at me, but as he swung with his arm, the bottle stayed stuck in his hand. His hand was wide open, but the bottle stayed stuck! He looked at his hand and tried to throw the bottle at me again, but it wouldn't come out of his hand!

The beer was wetting my face as he tried still a third time to hit me with it. He kept looking at the stuck bottle, wondering what was wrong. Then he really got angry and pointed the bottle in a different direction. As soon as he turned away from me, the bottle went right from his hand, hit the sidewalk, broke, and splattered beer and glass all over.

I know God had His angel there to protect me. As long as that bottle was pointed towards me, a child of God who is protected by Him, the angel said, "No way! This child belongs to God and you will not touch her or hurt her!" When you are out on the highways and byways of the world witnessing the love of Jesus to others, you are under divine protection!

I left him and went to work with other parts of my group. An hour later I came upon the same man again. By then God had sobered him up somewhat. Though he was still a little drunk, he was his own natural self. As I began to talk to him about Jesus, he said, "I'm really sorry I bothered your teenagers. I know better than that. Will you please forgive me?" "Yes," I said. "And do you know that Jesus loves you?" He said, "I don't think He really loves me anymore, but thanks for the sandwich."

I asked him if I could pray with him and he agreed. I prayed for God to strengthen him. Then I asked if he had ever asked the Lord into his heart. He told me he had, a long time ago.

The next day, Sunday, I preached in the church at the request of the pastor. It's a large church and while I was preaching, some of the teens in the congregation began pointing across the room and signaling me. When I looked towards the back door of the church, there was the man who had tried to hit me with a beer bottle!

As I watched, he started walking down the middle aisle. I thought he was looking for a seat but instead he kept walking straight towards me. When he got to me, he asked me if he could say something. I looked over towards the pastor to be sure it was all right to give him the microphone. The pastor agreed to what the Holy Spirit was already telling me.

The man took the mike, turned to the congregation, and said, "I've been a sinner. I used to be a pastor. I was a pastor for years. My wife ran off and had an affair, leaving me for another man. It broke my heart so badly that I had a nervous breakdown and just fell apart. Because of the breakdown, I was asked to leave and step down as pastor. That hurt me also. I decided no one loved me, not even God. I ended up on skid row."

"I've been out on the streets drinking since then. Yesterday, when your teens were out witnessing and sharing Scriptures, I started sharing Scriptures too. Then suddenly I felt the fire of God come back into me. I just want to come to church."

He began to sob, and then dropped to his knees, crying out, "Father, please forgive me! I've been a sinner! Bring me back to my calling! Bring me back to my first love! I want to get cleaned up and do Your will!"

God restored that drunken man just as He did the slave girl who had followed Paul! Paul commanded that spirit to come out of her in the name of Jesus Christ, and it came out. The same thing happened with the man in Seattle, when God used me to command a bad spirit to come out of him.

It's clear from the Scriptures that when we obey the leading of the Holy Spirit, God moves through us to see that people are saved and delivered.

When Paul and Silas changed their plans and went over to Macedonia, a woman named Lydia and her whole household were saved. A young slave girl was delivered from a bad spirit. God even worked through Lydia to provide Paul and Silas with a good living situation. However some other things happened too.

Some people in Macedonia got upset, especially when the slave girl got delivered . Her owners had been using her to make money at fortune telling. Soon they successfully conspired to have Paul and Silas thrown in jail for interfering with their livelihood!

> **But at midnight Paul and Silas were praying and singing hymns to God, and the prisoners were listening to them.** (Acts 16:25)

Scripture tells us that these men were not only thrown in jail. Before that, they were violently beaten, until their backs were bloody and ripped open. It was a situation where Silas might logically have wanted to tell Paul something like this: "Hey Paul, are you really sure you heard from the Holy Spirit about coming to this place?"

To this Paul might well have responded: "You know, Silas, ever since my dramatic experience with the Lord on the road to Damascus, things have been like this! Right in the middle of great blessings there have been times when one bad thing after another has happened!"

However Paul and Silas no longer responded according to human logic. With blood still dripping down their backs they sang out, "Thank You Jesus! Thank You Jesus! Lydia and her family got saved! The slave girl got saved and delivered! Jesus we thank You!"

They sang praise and thanksgiving to God for the souls that were saved through the Gospel that they faithfully preached. As they were singing, I personally believe God sent angels into that jail cell. Some angels were probably posted at the doors, others at the stockades and alongside the prisoners themselves. Those angels, under God's command, got everything into alignment for what was about to take place!

Suddenly there was a great earthquake, so that the foundations of the prison were shaken; and immediately all the doors were opened and everyone's chains were loosed.

And the keeper of the prison, awaking from sleep and seeing the prison doors open, sup-

> **posing the prisoners had fled, drew his sword and was about to kill himself. But Paul called with a loud voice saying, "Do yourself no harm, for we are all here."**
>
> **Then he called for a light, ran in, and fell down trembling before Paul and Silas. And he brought them out and said "Sirs, what must I do to be saved?"**
>
> **So they said, "Believe on the Lord Jesus Christ, and you will be saved, you and your household."** (Acts 16:26-31)

Isn't it amazing that suddenly the jailer came running to Paul and Silas asking about salvation? Though it's not stated in the Scripture, I'm certain that when Paul looked into the eyes of that man, he saw the person he'd seen in a vision weeks before, the man who had said, "Come to Macedonia and help us!"

I believe that all the other prisoners, who could have escaped, remained in their cells because God sent His angels. Powerful angels held on to each of them saying, "You're not going anywhere! The chains and shackles might be off you, but you're not leaving here until you hear the plan of salvation!" Otherwise those prisoners would have fled as soon as the cell doors opened.

The angels didn't let them go, because two of God's Spirit-led anointed ministers were there in the prison on assignment. God wanted everyone to be saved.

> **Then they spoke the word of the Lord to him and to all who were in his house. And he took them the same hour of the night and washed their stripes. And immediately he and all his family were baptized. Now when he had brought them into his house, he set food before them; and he rejoiced, having believed in God with all his household.** (Acts 16:32-34)

Paul preached Jesus to them all. The jailer and his whole family got saved. I believe everyone who heard the Gospel preached that night, including the prisoners, got saved also. Later on Paul and Silas met with the brethren at Lydia's house before continuing on their journey.

The obedience of one man, Paul, to hear the voice of the Holy Spirit, caused the birth of a church in Macedonia.

When we lift up Jesus, He will draw people to Himself. He said, **"And I, if I am lifted up from the earth, will draw all peoples to Myself."** (John 12:32)

Many Christians want to know, "How do you become a soul winner?"

Soul winning begins when you ask God to reveal His heart to you. And God's heart is for souls. That's what it's all about! **"For God so loved the world that He gave His only begotten Son..."** (John 3:16). God sent His Son, Jesus, to die on the cross so that the world could be saved from sin.

There is nothing more important than that the

people of God lead others to Christ. We are in the ministry of reconciliation. That means reconciling people back to Jesus.

As we are led by the same Holy Spirit who led Paul and Silas, much more can happen than we could ever imagine!

Chapter 7

Listen to the Holy Spirit!

As God's children we need to become very sensitive to the voice of the Holy Spirit. We need to be so confident in our ability to hear His voice (that still small voice on the inside of us), that when we hear, we will obey and take action as He directs. That's when we will always see the harvest of souls coming into the Kingdom, and people's lives changed.

The Gospels show us how this was exemplified in the lives of the disciples. In Luke chapter five, Jesus asked Simon Peter if he could use his fishing boat. Peter had been out fishing all night. Jesus wanted to preach from the boat so He had them push off a little from the shore.

> **When He had stopped speaking, He said to Simon, "Launch out into the deep and let down your nets for the catch."**
>
> **But Simon answered and said to Him, "Master, we have toiled all night and caught nothing; nevertheless at Your word I will let down the net."**
>
> (Luke 5:4-5)

With what we know of Simon Peter's rough character, it's conceivable that he may have thought, "Look,

Jesus, I'm the fisherman and You're the preacher. I'll let You use my boat to preach from, but don't tell me how to fish, and I won't tell You how to preach!"

Yet Peter had listened to Jesus preach. He saw something in Jesus; he sensed the anointing in Jesus. He sensed the Word of God. So he listened to Him. The Holy Spirit had already begun convincing Peter's heart.

He didn't ask Jesus a lot of questions. He simply said, **"We have toiled all night and caught nothing; nevertheless at Your word I will let down the net."**

> **And when they had done this, they caught a great number of fish, and their net was breaking. So they signaled to their partners in the other boat to come and help them. And they came and filled both the boats, so that they began to sink. When Simon Peter saw it, he fell down at Jesus' knees, saying, "Depart from me, for I am a sinful man, O Lord!"** (Luke 5:6-8)

When we come into the presence of God, we feel an awesome overwhelming presence. When the prophet Isaiah came into the presence of the Lord he cried out saying:

> **"Woe is me, for I am undone! Because I am a man of unclean lips, and I dwell in the midst of a people of unclean lips; for my eyes have seen the King, the Lord of hosts."** (Isaiah 6:5)

The good news of the Gospel of Jesus Christ is that God loves us even when we are sinners, and desires us to come to Jesus and be saved. God wants all of us to walk continually in His Holy Spirit, with His anointing upon us, hearing the voice of God.

Many of us have close, dearly loved friends and family members. Christians know the end is coming very soon. Everyone can see the prophetic signs coming to pass in the earth. We know that we all have special relatives, friends and acquaintances who are good people, but who need to come to a saving knowledge of Christ Jesus.

We need to know when, where, and how to let down our nets so that our loved ones and all those who are lost will come into the Kingdom. Peter toiled all night and caught nothing. But when the Lord spoke, Peter realized Who was speaking to him. Perhaps you have toiled for a long time in witnessing to a sister-in-law or brother-in-law, grandmother, son or co-worker.

Perhaps you have felt like you've just been hitting a hard wall. Nothing will come of your efforts. You may have cried to God, "I don't see anything happening!" You need to know that God says:

> **"So shall My word be that goes forth from My mouth; it shall not return to Me void, but it shall accomplish what I please, and it shall prosper in the thing for which I sent it. "**
>
> (Isaiah 55:11)

You can learn to hear the voice of God. When you pray, say, "Holy Spirit show me what has blocked this loved one from receiving You." The Holy Spirit will begin revealing things to you. It could be that the one you are praying for has been hurt by the church. It may be that they are confused, or were hurt as a child. The Holy Spirit can identify the problem, reveal exactly which tool to use, and show you how to share the love of Jesus with that person, so they can be saved. The process always involves reaching out in love.

We Are Your Help

Our ministry works with churches in the United States and world wide, doing citywide crusades. At one church, while out looking for a location for a city-wide crusade, the pastor and I were driving through the area when I suddenly heard the Holy Spirit say, "See that door over there? Go knock on that door." So I told the pastor we needed to go knock on the door of that small house. I felt a cry in my spirit.

The pastor asked me, "Do you know people who live here in town?" I told him no.

"Then how do you know you are supposed to knock at that door?" he asked. I said I was simply getting something from the Holy Spirit, telling me we needed to go there. "Well then, I need to go with you," he said.

He stopped the truck and we went up to the door and knocked. He asked me, "Do you have any idea what you're going to say yet, Sister Joan?" I had no idea. But I knew the Holy Spirit would tell me when the door opened.

It's not our word, but it's God's word when we hear the Lord. We're to do what the Holy Spirit says to do in that moment. God's word says, **"...Open thy mouth wide, and I will fill it."** (Psalm 81:10)

A woman opened the door. Suddenly out of my mouth came, "Hi! We're your help." She shouted to someone in the house, "Oh great! Honey, the help is here." She took the pastor and me by the hand and dragged us through the house saying, "Honey, the help is here. The help finally showed up!"

She had us sit in her little family room. I was thinking how awesome it was that she had brought us into her home.

I asked the Lord, "Holy Spirit what do You want me to say now?" The Holy Spirit said, "Share Jesus with them."

Remember, the greatest help you can give to anyone in this world is to bring them to Jesus. When they come to know Jesus as their Lord and Savior, they will have the friend who will be with them all their lives. Jesus will be there for their healing, their finances, their marriages, their children, or whatever is needed. Jesus is the answer the world needs to hear!

I said to the woman, "The greatest help I can give

you and your husband is to introduce you to Jesus Christ. He's my best friend."

The pastor and I began taking them through the scriptures, **"line upon line and precept upon precept"** (Isaiah 28:9-10)**.** Then I shared with them about how God loves them, and went on to salvation scriptures. After that I asked if they would like to pray and invite Jesus into their hearts. They looked at one another. The wife said she wanted to, and then the husband said yes, too. We all joined hands together and we prayed. They asked Jesus into their hearts, inviting Him to be their Lord and Savior.

After we prayed, I asked the woman about what happened when we came to her door. "What did you need help with?"

"Didn't the lady from the welfare office send you here," she asked. When I said no, she told me they had gone to the welfare office earlier that day to get food and assistance with their electric bill. The welfare office had rejected them. They owned a home and car, which disqualified them from receiving public assistance.

They had headed back to the parking lot, looking rather sad and depressed. A woman in the lot must have noticed, because she came over to them and said, "You look as if you've just lost your best friend!" They told her about their need. She asked them for their name and address, telling them that she couldn't promise anything, but would see if her church might be able to help.

She asked them if she could pray with them. Then right in that parking lot that woman prayed, "Father in Heaven, they need help. Please, dear God, send them help. You know their situation and what they need. So please send them help."

The wife asked me if the woman in the parking lot had given us their name and address. I had to tell her I didn't know anything about the woman or the welfare office. She asked me how I knew to knock on her door. I told her we were in the area and the Holy Spirit of God directed us to knock on her door.

God had heard the prayer asking for help that was said in the welfare office parking lot. God heard their prayer and then spoke to my heart to knock on their door and say, "Hi, we are your help. Your help is here."

God looks at your heart and knows your needs. He sees, hears, and knows your heart cry and your prayers. He will send people to help you!

It's so wonderful to know that you can hear God and obey Him. When you do that, lives are changed; people are saved, healed, delivered and blessed!

Chapter 8

Listening: A Personal Testimony

Let me tell you a personal experience I had where God really put me to the test about obeying His will. He asked me to do something very difficult. He will surely put you to the test too. What joy when we hear Him and obey Him!

Lord, my house?

One day I took a group of people from my hometown out witnessing. I was teaching them how to witness in an area where there were prostitutes and gang members. I heard the Holy Spirit say, "You see the lady getting ready to walk into that bar? Go over and talk to her." So I walked up to the woman, who was obviously a prostitute working the streets. I handed her a tract and began talking to her about Jesus.

Her immediate response was, "Look, lady, I know where all the churches are. If I want somebody to preach to me, I know where to go. I'll go on my own."

"No you won't," I said. "Yeah, well if I want somebody to preach to me, I could just turn on the Christian radio station or something. Why are you out here anyway?" I told her, "Because Jesus said we need to help people." She said, "Yeah. Yeah. Yeah. You guys want to help people. You want to help get us off the street." "Yeah, that's right," I said.

She went on to say, "I know how you all are! You want to get me off the streets and then take me to church with you on Sunday, so that everybody can say, 'Look what she did. She's got points in heaven now!' All you want is points! You think if you get enough little points you get to go to heaven! You don't really care about us!"

I turned inward and asked, "Lord, do I really care?" And the Lord said to me, "Invite her home." I said, "Lord, do you mean my house!" I told her, "Look, you can come home with me and live with me if you want to get off the streets."

"Oh really? For how long?" she asked. I asked the Lord and he said for however long it would take. He said I should take her into my home until she was rooted and grounded in the Word of God and able to take care of herself.

At the same time the Lord was speaking to me, I had a vision. I saw my microwave disappearing, and my stereo, my jewelry, my TV and VCR, all disappearing. The Lord saw this vision too! In fact He gave me the vision.

The Lord asked me, "What is more important to you? Your things, or being obedient to me?" I immediately responded. I said to the woman, "You can come and live with me for however long it takes."

Her response was, "Why would you do that lady?"

This is what I told her.

"I'll tell you why I would do such a thing. I know a woman who was twenty-three years old when she made wrong choices in life. She had run away from home at the age of eighteen because she was sexually abused and beaten. That woman was me."

"By the age of twenty three, I had two babies and was pregnant with a third. More terrible things happened. I was literally thrown out of the place where I was staying and was out on the streets homeless."

As I was telling all this to the prostitute, she began crying. She told me, "I don't want to hear anymore, lady! You're making me mess up my mascara. I've got to work tonight, and I don't want to hear any more of your story!"

"You're going to hear the rest of my story," I said, and I kept right on talking.

"There I was out in the rain in Portland, Oregon. I was pregnant and bruised, with two babies screaming and crying. I was illiterate, unable to read and write. I couldn't even use a phone book, since I didn't know how to read. I had $1.50 in my pocket.

"I gathered up my stuff which had been thrown out on the porch of the house where I'd been living. Then I stuck things in a bag and grabbed my two children.

"I got inside the nearest phone booth, to get us out of the rain. I stood there, and I cried out, saying, 'God, if you're real and if there really is a God in heaven, and all this stuff I heard as a child about God and Jesus is real, then I need to hear from you right now! Help me please.'"

The prostitute was really crying now. She kept saying she didn't want to hear any more, but I continued.

"In that phone booth, I heard a voice from heaven say, 'Remember the lady at the donut shop? Call her.'"

"A few days before I'd met a lady there who'd given me a little card. I dialed the number on the card and told the person who answered, 'Look, I don't know how to read or write and I can't use the phone book. Tell me how to call the Battered Women's place or Welfare, or do something so I can get me and my babies off the street.'"

"The woman I spoke with told me to go to the donut shop and wait for her. I told her I only had $1.50 in my pocket. She told me to just go there and order something for the children. She would be there to get me in forty-five minutes."

"That woman, a total stranger, came and took me and my children off the streets and helped me. She was there when I gave birth to my daughter. She counseled me to keep my baby, rather than put her up for adoption. She said, 'Joan, you already have two, one more won't hurt.'"

"I'm so glad I kept my daughter. She's a joy to me, as are my boys! God took me off the streets when

I needed help. People helped me get financial aid and baby clothes. Total strangers helped me get food and cribs for the babies. They helped me!"

I looked at this young prostitute and told her, "That's why I'll help you. I want you to know that you are welcome in my house for as long as it takes."

Just then her "man" came over and yelled at me to stop messing around with his girl. She immediately followed him into the bar.

I followed her in and gave her a booklet about Jesus. I told her, "Jesus loves you. There's a better way!" I put the booklet right in her hand and told her my name and phone number were printed on the back. If she changed her mind, she could call me. My offer still stood.

"I went back outside to my group. They joined hands with me to pray. Her name was Cobra and we prayed for her salvation and the power of God to convict her. We prayed a long time and then I told the group to go home. Then I went home and sat in my rocking chair, rocking and praying for hours. Finally, at 5:00 a.m., I crawled into bed, still thinking about Cobra and praying.

Suddenly the phone rang. It was her!

"Are you serious about taking me in?" she asked.

I told her I was.

She said she was in a phone booth and gave me the address.

Fifteen minutes later, this young prostitute named

Cobra was in my car. She told me, "I'm going to be a hard case to deal with. I'm hooked on cocaine. I want to know what you did to me tonight lady!"

I asked her what she meant, and she said, "I took some cocaine tonight. I always do, because I can't stand what I do. I know it's wrong.

"I waited for the cocaine to work, but it didn't. I thought they sold me some bad stuff, you know? So I got some more. But that didn't work either.

"All I kept hearing all night is, 'Jesus loves you. There's a better way!' I kept hearing it over and over again. All I could hear was your voice saying that.

"I couldn't take it anymore. So I grabbed my bag of clothes and went to the phone booth. I'm going to be hard to live with, but I'm going to try."

When we went to church Sunday morning, she said, "I'm going to sit here in back because I'm not dressed too proper."

It didn't matter where she sat, right there in the back of the church the Spirit of the Lord came upon her. Suddenly she got up and ran to the front. The pastor was in the middle of leading praise and worship, and she literally grabbed the microphone out of his hand.

"I'm a sinner, a prostitute and a junkie," she told us. "I lost my children because of drugs." Then she dropped to her knees, saying, "I want Jesus!" She wept and cried and received Jesus Christ as her Lord and Savior.

Immediately the congregation went wild, praising and worshipping God!

Jesus said, **"I say to you likewise there will be more joy in heaven over one sinner who repents..."** (Luke 15:7). There is joy in heaven over one!

That's what it's all about! Aren't you ready to hear the voice of God? Aren't you ready to hear and obey the voice of the Holy Spirit? Then allow the Holy Spirit to lead you, no matter how hard it might seem, even to the point of taking a stranger into your home.

No matter how odd it may seem in the natural, when you are hearing and obeying the voice of the Holy Spirit, it is God who will use you!

 **Now is the time to let God use you!**

Chapter 9

Lifting Up Jesus

As you can see from the last story, God has sometimes used me in a peculiar way, and not with enticing words of human wisdom.

> **And I brethren, when I came to you, did not come with excellence of speech or of wisdom declaring to you the testimony of God. For I determined not to know anything among you except Jesus Christ and Him crucified.**
>
> **I was with you in weakness, in fear, and in much trembling. And my speech and my preaching were not with persuasive words of human wisdom, but in demonstration of the Spirit and of power, that your faith should not be in the wisdom of men but in the power of God.** (1Corinthians 2:1-5)

When God called me into ministry, I could not read. I was illiterate. God supernaturally taught me to read! For a time, I still stumbled through, especially if I read too quickly. When I first began preaching the Gospel, just like Paul said to the people of Corinth in this Scripture, I did not have enticing words of human wisdom.

One time as I was preaching, I noticed the pastor whispering something to his wife, and she laughed. She leaned over and spoke to the person next to her and soon everyone in the front row was laughing. When we went out to lunch after the service, I asked the pastor why they'd been laughing. He said, "Sister Joan, you are so cute. When you read that one Scripture, you pointed out that Jesus came to save the Republicans and the sinners. What it really says is, 'publicans and sinners'. It seems that you just kind of dissect words and make up some new ones!"

On another occasion I was preaching from the book of Daniel and I said soul winners were like the "figment" of the stars. A woman came up to me later and asked, "What in the world is a 'figment'?" I told her, "Oh well, you know there in Daniel 12:3, it says, 'Those who are wise shall shine like the brightness of the figment.'" She said, "Oh honey, that doesn't say 'figment', it says, 'firmament'." I just said, "Oh."

Even if I was not getting some of the words right, people were still getting saved! Even if I wasn't sure what I was doing, people still received Jesus. Those people weren't looking at a person and how she was messing up her words. They were looking at the heart.

When you begin witnessing and telling people about Jesus, you should never tell them you don't know enough about the Scriptures or that you can't pronounce this word or that word. You shouldn't worry about any of that. God Almighty is looking at your heart. He will take you and use the very simplicity of your heart. The heart-felt prayer, the heart that says, "I want to see people get saved," is what God will use.

Just as the apostle Paul told the people of Corinth, all you need to do is share Jesus Christ and Him crucified.

Your Jesus

Early in my Christian walk, I was helping to teach people how to do door to door witnessing. Many churches in our area came together to do a soul-winning seminar. On Saturday, the final day, we met to prepare to go out on the streets. Because it was in the middle of winter, we were all dressed in heavy, warm clothing.

The Holy Spirit directed me to an area where I came upon a man standing in his driveway, who was working on his car. He had the hood up and car parts were strewn all over the place. I walked over to him and commented about his having car problems. He said, "Yes lady, I'm having car problems." I noticed he spoke with an accent, so I said, "I can detect from your accent that you're from a different country." He told me that he was Vietnamese. He'd been in the United States for a year.

I said, "That's wonderful! You've only been in our country a year and you already know how to drive and fix cars." He said, "No lady, I don't know how to fix cars. I only know how to take them apart! I'm trying to figure out how to put all these parts back in, because I don't remember where they go."

I said to him, "I can pray for you! My Jesus can help you remember where you took the parts out so that you can put them back in." Meanwhile I was thinking, "This is a crazy way to evangelize, using the car as a way to get someone saved." It didn't seem to make sense, and even seemed very foolish.

The man said he was a Buddhist. I told him, "You know what? I just came back from India where we prayed for people with blind eyes. Can your Buddha heal blind eyes?" He said, "No." Ever so proudly I said, "My Jesus can!"

As we talked, I happened to glance over to the side and saw a man taking out a bag of garbage, and the Holy Spirit said, "Go over and take that man by the arm." I walked over to him, took him by the arm, and said, "Come over here, sir. You need to hear what I have to say." I led him to the car repairman's drive-way. With my hands on his shoulders I said, "Now you just listen to what I have to say."

I turned my back on him and continued talking to the other man saying, "While I was in India we prayed for lepers and Jesus healed them. Can your Buddha heal lepers?" He said, "No." I said, "My Jesus can!"

Then I told him, "There were people with deaf-ness in their ears. Can your Buddha heal deaf ears?" He said, "No." I said again, "My Jesus can!"

Nine times I called out different diseases the Lord healed. Each time, like a proud little child, I said, "My Jesus can!"

I thought the way I was witnessing was so crazy and strange, but the Word of God says, **"For as the heavens are higher than the earth, so are My ways higher than your ways, and My thoughts than your thoughts"** (Isaiah 55:9).

The Word also says,

"But God has chosen the foolish things of the world to put to shame the wise; and God has chosen the weak things of the world to put to shame the things which are mighty...." (1Corinthians 1:27)

I wasn't sure what God was doing. I only knew that I wanted to be obedient to how His Spirit was leading. Soon the man with the car said, "Look lady, I really don't care what your Jesus can do. I'm trying to fix my car. Would you just go away."

I said, "Okay, I'll go away, but I want to give you this little book I wrote called *The Empty Spot*. As I put the book on his fender, I mentioned I'd written my phone number in it in case he wanted to know more about Jesus.

I also turned to the man standing behind me. Since he hadn't said a word, and looked Vietnamese, I wondered if he could speak or understand English. I gave him a book too, and told him to call me if he wanted to know more about Jesus.

I went along my way and continued passing out tracts. Then I rejoined the group from the church. Everyone had wonderful witnessing testimonies. I thought I really didn't have a testimony, because I'd just passed out tracts and given out a few books, and I hadn't led anyone to the Lord.

Later I realized that I shouldn't have judged by immediate results. Just because you don't see an instant change, doesn't mean that something hasn't happened. When you leave a tract tucked in a doorway, or talk with someone about the Lord, you may never know how the Holy Spirit used what you did. We may never know until we get to Heaven. Then people will come over to you saying, "Hey! Remember me? You gave me a tract that told me about our Lord!" Or, "I'm the one you sat next to on the train that day, and you told me about Jesus."

A few days after I'd spoken with those Vietnamese men, I received a phone call. "Hello, is this Mrs. Joan? I read your book over and over. Did you get my letter? You told me that if I wanted to know more about this Jesus man to give you a call. I want to know more about this Jesus man."

I arranged to meet with him the next morning, accompanied by my friend Ann. It's wise to always minister as a team.

Later that day, I received his letter. "Dear Lady Joan", he wrote "I read your book *The Empty Spot* over and over. I do not understand this little book. The words on the paper floated like little feathers into my heart the more I read it."

The whole book consists of Scriptures on how to get saved.

His letter went on to say, "The end of the book says you pray and ask this Jesus man to come into your heart to be your Lord and Savior. Please come quick! Words cannot explain on paper what happened to me."

When Ann and I met him the next morning, he wanted to tell us his story. During the Vietnam War he had worked on the American side with the Americans. As a high official in the military, he was captured and put in a prisoner of war camp.

Because he was considered to have a lot of "information in his head, " he was often tortured. We cried as he told us how he had screamed in intense pain. He spread out his hands and showed us how his fingernails were ripped out with pliers. He didn't have one fingernail left.

Though He hadn't known to whom he was praying, he said he kept crying out, "Oh Power higher than Buddha, please help me!"

One time he was placed into a bamboo tank where only his head was above water, and his hands were handcuffed behind his back. He was left there for 3 days and nights. Leeches stuck to his body, sucking his blood. The only way he could stand the intense pain was to pray, "Oh Power higher than Buddha, help me!"

He was tortured that way for years and he continued praying those words, never really knowing to whom he was praying. One night he escaped from the camp. He traveled through the jungle, never knowing when he might step on a land mine or booby trap.

Tired and in constant pain, he continued praying the same way, "Power higher than Buddha, help me!"

He told us that when I took him by the arm and brought him over to where his friend was fixing his car, all he could hear of what I was saying was, "Jesus, Jesus, Jesus." He heard me say Jesus nine times.

He had walked away with my book in his hand, knowing that it was Jesus who had led him to safely through the jungle. "It was your Jesus, who was the Power higher than Buddha, who saved and protected me."

Suddenly my sense of how foolish I'd felt while witnessing to those Vietnamese men didn't matter at all. Through hearing the name of Jesus nine times, the man who had cried out to the "Power higher than Buddha" while in that prisoner of war camp, was finally introduced to the One he had cried out to. He got to meet Jesus, and was able to receive Him as his Lord and Savior. Because someone followed the leading of the Holy Spirit a soul was saved. That's what matters!

As that Vietnamese man went through very troubled times, God heard his desperate cries and helped him. Surely we are living today in perilous times and many reading this book have been crying out for help too.

If you are not certain you have fully committed your life to Jesus, now is the time. If you want to receive Jesus into your heart or renew your commitment to Jesus, now is the time.

Pray this prayer to Jesus, meaning it with your whole heart:

> *Jesus, I am sorry for my sins. I ask you to come into my life and help me to follow you and serve you. Come into my heart now dear Jesus. Thank you for saving my soul.*

 **The seed you sow for souls will grow!**

Chapter 10

Soul Winner's Crown

Because of our great love for Jesus, we don't want to go before the throne of the King of kings and Lord of lords empty handed. We are saved when we ask Jesus into our hearts, but it's possible to go to Heaven empty-handed. We want to have something to lay at the feet of Jesus. God has made it possible for us to have gifts to bring. There are different rewards that we can receive, and one of them is a soul winner's crown.

Scripture tells us with great clarity, that one day every person who ever lived or will live on the earth will bow down and confess Jesus Christ as Lord. However they will bow down from different places.

> **Let this mind be in you which was also in Christ Jesus, who, being in the form of God, did not consider it robbery to be equal with God, but made Himself of no reputation, taking the form of a bondservant, and coming in the likeness of men.**
>
> **And being found in appearance as a man, He humbled Himself and became obedient to the point of death, even the death of the cross.**
>
> **Therefore God also has highly exalted Him and given Him the name which is above every name, that at the name of Jesus every knee should bow,**

> **of those in heaven, and of those on earth, and of those under the earth, and that every tongue should confess that Jesus Christ is Lord, to the glory of God the Father.** (Philippians 2:5-11)

How enormously important it is that we be in the right place when we kneel before our beloved King!

All the angels, the twenty-four elders, and all the saints of God who have gone to be with the Lord will bow down in heaven. (See Revelation 4:10, and 5:11-12, and 7:11-14.)

All those who are on the earth and know Jesus will also kneel and say the same thing. When Jesus enters as King of kings and Lord of lords they will be saying, **"Worthy is the Lamb of God."**

People who are under the earth will cry out too, but with a different cry. Among them will be those who have received the mark of the beast, along with the false prophet. (See Revelation 19:20 and 20:10.)

Even as they bow their knees they will be weeping in agony, as they acknowledge that Jesus is Lord and Savior. In horrible turmoil they will realize they've chosen not to be with Jesus, but it will be too late for them to change their minds. Even Lucifer (Satan) will formally acknowledge he has lost. Jesus has won.

On that day when we who love and serve the Lord Jesus stand before our Savior, what a joy it will be to remove our soul winner's crowns from our heads and cast them in loving adoration at the feet of our beloved Lord.

God has made a way for us to receive a crown to lay at the feet of Jesus. It is a crown made by adding precious souls to His Kingdom. It signifies that we have obeyed the Great Commission of our King (Matthew 28:19-20), and let people know about Jesus while there is still time. There is a work for all of God's people, leading others to Christ.

The Vision

I learned about the soul winner's crown from the Lord, in an unusual way. It's a story I am somewhat ashamed to tell. However I'm going to be honest about it, because I sense in my spirit there are people who need to hear it.

I was doing missionary work in a dangerous Communist-ruled area in the mountains of Mexico. Our team had been warned about strong anti-Christian activity, which had led to the murder of some nearby missionaries. Their bodies were found in a gully. We were told if our evangelistic activities were discovered our lives were in physical danger. For safety, we were to remain close to the house where we were staying.

One day, I was out walking and praying. Off in the distance I saw jeeps coming that had swastikas and communist flags on them. Thinking it wasn't quite time for me to die or be martyred, I jumped into the bushes to hide until they drove by.

While I was hiding in the bushes, the Lord gave me an open vision. It was the kind of vision I've rarely experienced. I saw myself with a soul winner's crown on my head. It was absolutely beautiful. It had diamonds, emeralds, sapphires and other kinds of stones, some I couldn't even recognize. It was gold, which had a luster beyond anything I'd ever seen. The colors on the crown were so radiant that the light reflecting off of it seemed alive.

Suddenly, the crown rolled off my head and fell into a mud puddle. It sat on top of the mud for a second or two, and as I watched, every one of the stones dropped out of the crown and sank into the mud. The crown sat there empty for a moment, and then also sank in the mud.

"Oh Lord!" I cried out, "What are You trying to show me?" I was already aware of how the Lord chastises those He loves. It never feels good to be spanked by God.

The Lord answered, "Joan, you've been a missionary for years. You've done a lot of great things and have led many people to Me. But your heart isn't right before Me."

When I asked Him to explain He said, "You wanted recognition from man. You wanted people saved, but you wanted to promote yourself. You've wanted to write in your newsletters how many were saved, and healed, and how large your crusades were. You've been doing things from another motive, rather than the pure motive of seeing souls come into My Kingdom. You have wanted to be somebody."

The only possible response was, "You are right Lord. I have been trying to be somebody."

After the Lord spanked me, He said, "Because of your wrong heart attitude, your reward is gone." Suddenly I lost all track of time.

"Oh Lord," I sobbed, "please forgive me. Please fix my heart. Make my motives pure so that I won't stretch the truth about how many got saved or healed, or how big the crusades were. Make me a vessel of honor and glory for You alone, Lord."

Suddenly the Lord asked, "Will you do it My way, Joan?"

I said, "Yes Lord, I will!" I rejoiced that God would give me another chance. The God we serve is the God of another chance.

As you are reading this, you may be thinking you've done something wrong and that God will not forgive you for it. Perhaps you've even shut down your ministry because of it. I want you to know that all you have to do is repent to the Lord. Just tell Him you are sorry, and God will pick you up in His arms. He will love you and direct you and help you to get you back on course. That is what the Lord did for me.

As soon as I repented the Lord said, "Are you ready to do it My way, Joan? Will you allow Me to put the stones in your soul winners crown, and stop trying to do it yourself?"

I said, "Yes, Lord, I will."

Again I saw the Lord's hand go over the mud puddle and the crown came out of the water and up into Jesus' hand. It came up totally clean. The beautiful gold shone, though it was still empty of stones. I was so happy when I felt Jesus come over to me, replace the crown on my head, and press it down over my forehead.

Next in the vision, the Lord took me to Heaven. I was like a little girl all excited about a party; that's the only way I can describe it. I felt electric excitement in the air, just everywhere! It was so awesome.

A voice asked, "Are you ready, Joan?"

I looked to my left, and there stood a thirteen or fourteen foot tall angel. He walked over to me with the soul winner's crown, but now it was filled with all its stones, just as I'd seen it in the vision, before it fell into the mud. As he placed it on my head I was like a little girl all excited with this crown on my head. I was totally filled with the love of God. The atmosphere of Heaven is pure love beyond words!

I saw another huge angel with a long, gold horn in his hand. As he blew it, the sound went everywhere!

They asked, "Are you ready?"

Unsure about what was ahead, I responded, "I guess so."

A door was opened, and an angel said, "You can go in now."

I walked past the entrance into the presence of the Lord. Immediately I dropped to my knees. Taking the crown off of my head, I threw it at the feet of Jesus, saying, "You are worthy! You are worthy!"

I remain, even today, in amazement at God's awesome presence and amazing love.

Even here on earth, people who go into the presence of a king bring gifts. The wise men came to Israel looking for a king. When they found the one they were seeking, they brought out gifts and laid them at the feet of the child Jesus.

> **....And when they had opened their treasures, they presented gifts to Him: gold, frankincense, and myrrh.** (Matthew 2:11)

When we go to Heaven, we can take nothing from this earth with us. We come into the world naked and naked we go out. God has given us a way to receive crowns to lay at His feet.

We need to be soul winners and tell everyone about Jesus, but our heart attitude has to be right before God. At one time, my heart attitude was rotten. It stunk. But God corrected the attitude of my heart. Now, my heart truly is to see people saved. I have no other motive than their being in Heaven, knowing Jesus as Lord and Savior.

I am so thankful that Jesus saved me. As you're

reading this you too may be thankful for your salvation. The way to show our gratitude and appreciation is to take the Gospel, the Good News that was given to us, to this lost and dying world. That way they can know Jesus too.

Your Soul Winner's Crown is your treasure to lay before our KING OF KINGS!

Chapter 11

Be A Light

Each of us, deep in our hearts, desires to have souls daily added to our soul winner's crowns. We want to be a light in this dark world. But how? The apostle Paul gives us some direction. The process involves obedience to the Holy Spirit, who has been given from God to help us be a light.

> **Therefore, my beloved, as you have always obeyed, not as in my presence only, but now much more in my absence, work out your own salvation with fear and trembling; for it is God who works in you both to will and to do for His good pleasure.**
>
> **Do all things without complaining and disputing, that you may become blameless and harmless, children of God without fault in the midst of a crooked and perverse generation, among whom you shine as lights in the world, holding fast the word of life, so that I may rejoice in the day of Christ that I have not run in vain or labored in vain.**
>
> (Philippians 2:12-16)

You are called to be lights, sharing the plan of salvation. Your only reason for being on earth is so that all will see Jesus and come to Him. Everything on earth produces after its own kind. Corn seeds produce corn, cats produce cats, and Christians produce Christians. That's just the plan of God. However the more we understand God's plan and walk in it, the more fruitful we will be.

Christians don't get saved simply to go to Heaven. If that were God's plan, the best time to die would be just after we are saved and baptized. The minister would baptize someone, put them under the water saying, "I baptize you in the name of the Father, Son, and Holy Spirit," and wait to hear the "glug, glug, glug" sound as the new convert drowned. That way there would be no backslidden Christians!

Certainly, the most important thing about our salvation is that we'll go to Heaven and be with God forever. However, God's salvation plan involves much more than saving your soul.

When you invite Jesus to be Lord of your life, you become part of God's family. It then becomes your responsibility to join with your brothers and sisters, and bring others into His family! That's how you become fruitful for God. That's when your light will shine out into this crooked, perverse and dark generation.

Jesus humbled Himself and became obedient, even to the point of death on the Cross, to bring about salvation for all the world. Likewise, we, God's children, need to be obedient to the Great Commission, which is a mandate to share Jesus.

We are to go out to the highways and byways of the world and compel the people to come to the saving knowledge of Jesus. We can compel them by continuing to love them, talk to them and pray for them. We are not to yell and scream at them; we are to simply love them and share the Scriptures with them as the Holy Spirit leads.

The Bible has a sense of urgency when it says, **"Behold, now is the accepted time; behold, now is the day of salvation"** (2Corinthians 6:2).

Thank God that He sent His Son Jesus, and that He was obedient to the point of death on the cross. Without His death on the cross, there would not be a way for us to get to Heaven. Jesus went into the holy of holies and sprinkled His Blood on the mercy seat so that we can be redeemed and receive salvation and abide in His love, peace, happiness, and joy all the days of our lives.

> **But Christ came as High Priest of the good things to come, with the greater and more perfect tabernacle not made with hands, that is not of this creation. Not with the blood of goats and calves, but with His own blood He entered the Most Holy Place once for all, having obtained eternal redemption.**
>
> (Hebrews 9:11-12)

Philippians 4:7 says we can have the **"peace of God, which surpasses all understanding."** There are people all over the world who are searching for peace in their lives. They try to find it in many ways, such as by spending money on fancy trips, houses and clothing, or by striving for success. But, inner peace is **only** found in knowing Jesus.

If you aren't experiencing the peace of God in your life, you can pray right now. Open your heart and acknowledge that you need the Lord to help you, and that you are a sinner, for we all have made mistakes.

Just say,
"Dear Jesus, I am sorry for all the sins I have done in my life. Thank you for forgiving me. Thank you for dying on the cross of Calvary for me. I ask you to come into my life. Be my savior. Take total control of my life. And I will follow You, love You and obey You all the days of my life." Amen.

Chapter 12

Life and Death Are in the Balance

You never know when someone's life, or even your own life, literally hangs in the balance. Especially in these last days, life itself may depend upon our ability to hear and follow the voice of the Holy Spirit. We can trust God to guide and protect us. The Holy Spirit may direct us to change our driving route, rearrange our scheduled shopping trip, or choose a different restaurant for lunch. Only when we get to Heaven will we know how much inconvenience and even danger we've avoided by listening to and obeying the leading of the Holy Spirit.

Recent horrible events such as terrorist attacks in New York City and Washington, D.C., random drive-by shootings, people being hit on the head while walking to work, and children shot in schools, highlight the seriousness of our situation. As people in the world become crazier and more depraved, we desperately need the wisdom of God to guide us in our daily lives.

God's people must stay built up in the Holy Spirit. Our lives and the lives of others are at stake.

But you, beloved, [build] yourselves up on your most holy faith, praying in the Holy Spirit....
(Jude 20)

Just before Jesus ascended into Heaven after His resurrection, He told His disciples:

> **"But you shall receive power when the Holy Spirit has come upon you; and you shall be witnesses to Me in Jerusalem, and in all Judea and Samaria, and to the end of the earth."**
>
> (Acts 1:8)

Jesus gave them, and us, clear directions for ministry. Where do you begin witnessing? Right in your hometown, then in your country, and then in the outermost parts of the world.

The Holy Spirit teaches us how to become witnesses; He fills us with the miracle power of God. To receive all that the Holy Spirit has for us, we must become sensitive to His voice. I want to tell you a personal story about my son and me.

I was a fairly new Christian when I moved to Kennewick, Washington. I didn't know many people in the area, but one of the women I worked with invited me to attend a "Women's Aglow" retreat. I'd recently received the baptism of the Holy Spirit, and thought it would be nice to attend a Christian weekend seminar.

During the first evening service, I began feeling an unexplainable inner heaviness, accompanied by a strong urge to cry. I felt grievious sorrow and pain, as if someone was hurting or dying. Without knowing what, I knew something was definitely wrong.

One women from our group sensed my mood, and asked me if I was okay. After assuring her I was fine, I went to my room to spend some time alone in prayer. "Oh, God what's wrong? I prayed. Have I sinned against You?" My first thought was that perhaps I'd grieved the Holy Spirit in some way, so I repented of everything I could think of!

There was a powerful speaker at the Saturday morning service and I really enjoyed her message. Yet even then, I caught myself sobbing once in awhile. The women I'd come with noticed me wiping away tears, and commented that I seemed a little strange. I said I knew something was wrong, but I didn't know what it was. Mostly I tried to suppress my odd and sad feelings.

By the evening service, my heaviness was dramatically increasing. Not wanting to make a scene, I sat at the back of meeting room. By the end of the service I felt like I would burst. Tears running down my face, I got up to go to my room, hoping I'd get there before I totally lost it. My sudden dash out of the meeting attracted some attention. Bless God for those saints who followed me out, to make sure I was all right!

As I walked across the lobby, I was hit so hard that cries came out. Feeling very faint, I knelt down by one of the sofas, put my head down and cried. Soon I was at a point where no words were coming out of my mouth.

> **Likewise the Spirit also helps in our weaknesses. For we do not know what we should pray for as we ought, but the Spirit Himself makes intercession for us with groanings which cannot be uttered.**
>
> **Now He who searches the hearts knows what the mind of the Spirit is, because He makes intercession for the saints according to the will of God.**
>
> **And we know that all things work together for good to those who love God, to those who are called according to His purpose.**
>
> (Romans 8:26-28)

Though I didn't realize it then, the Holy Spirit was groaning through me. Soon I was unable to pray in English, or in the Holy Spirit. I knelt there groaning in travail and pain, with no idea of what was happening to me.

Some ladies went and got some pastors who were seminar advisors. One of them laid hands on me. "Sister Joan," he said, "pray in the Holy Ghost! Pray in tongues, and ask the Holy Spirit to reveal to you what is happening!" As a small group surrounded me, praying, I began praying in tongues. Though I couldn't speak in English, my mind kept saying, "Show me, Holy Spirit!"

Suddenly I envisioned my fifteen-year-old son committing suicide. I screamed, "No, Rob. No! Don't kill yourself! No, Rob! No! My son has a suicide spirit trying to kill him!"

My scream was so loud a hotel staff member told them, "You've got to get this lady out of the lobby. You're making a scene!" Two women helped me up, and walked me back to my room. I was too weak to walk alone, and was still praying in the Spirit.

As the service ended, women came to ask what was happening. When told about my vision of my son trying to kill himself, about thirty women came into my hotel room. "Sister," they said, "we are going to pray and stand in the gap with you. This could be one of our own children."

We prayed in the Holy Spirit as God directed, letting the Holy Spirit make intercession according to God's will. I called home to find out where Rob was, but no one knew.

It turned out there'd been a huge fight and he'd run away from home that night. The Holy Spirit would not allow me to pack up and leave. He just kept me there on my face praying and groaning, until 5:30 Sunday morning. When the Holy Spirit finally told me that I could go, the women helped me throw my stuff into my car. I drove home as fast as I could.

Two hours later, I was home and went straight to my son's bedroom. I had to see him alive. I did not want to find out that he was dead. As I walked into his room, my tall, skinny fifteen-year-old boy was standing there. I wrapped my arms around him, just saying his name over and over again. Wrapped in each other's arms, we just cried together.

A spirit of suicide had attacked my son. Through prayer, angels had been sent on assignment to rescue him. Rob had not yet received Jesus as his Lord and Savior. Had he died that night he would have gone to hell.

Two weeks later, I went to Utah to visit my sister who had been in a serious car accident. Rob was still somewhat depressed. I didn't want to leave him home alone, so he went with me. As we drove, I played a Bible cassette with someone reading the book of Revelation.

I was in the fast lane, when Rob grabbed my arm and demanded that I pull the car over. He turned around in the front seat, got on his knees, and said, "I want to invite Jesus into my heart right now. I don't have time to wait! I have to do it right now!" I managed to get across the lanes and pull the car over. Rob prayed and asked Jesus into his heart there on the side of the highway.

I thank God the whole ordeal with my son taught me just how important it is to listen to the voice of the Holy Spirit. When He tells us something is not right, we need to heed His leading. Sensitivity to the Holy Spirit is a life and death matter!

Gypsy Boy

We were preaching at a small Gypsy church in California, where there was a group of somewhat rebellious teenagers. When I was preaching Sunday morning, a whole row of them sat at the back of the church leaning back in their chairs. They were laughing, giggling at me, and sending notes back and forth. I couldn't help thinking, "How rude those teens are."

Later, my husband and I prayed for their lives and their salvation. We knew that God wanted them saved.

During the Monday evening service, they were just as rude as can be, but the Holy Spirit told me to have them all sit in the front. Right in the middle of preaching, the Holy Spirit said, "Right now they are ready to receive Me as Lord and Savior!" I turned to them and said, "All of you teenagers join hands. The Lord is saying that you are ready to pray and ask Jesus into your hearts!"

They all looked up at me and I asked, "Are you ready?" They all nodded their heads. Some had tears in their eyes. I led the entire group in prayer to receive the Lord.

The following night, I was just getting up to preach when one of the boys walked up right in front of me. I asked him what he wanted.

"I want the baptism of the Holy Ghost," he said, "and I don't want to wait until you're done preaching. I don't want to wait for an altar call, I want the baptism now!"

As I went to pray for him, the Holy Spirit revealed that the prayer wasn't to be just for him, but for all the teens, and others too.

I explained to the congregation how the Holy Spirit would come upon them as on the day of Pentecost, to fill them with the fire of God, the very presence and anointing of His Spirit.

When I asked if anyone else wanted to receive the baptism of the Holy Spirit, the entire youth group came forward and the altar area was filled with people, young and old. They prayed and received the baptism and began speaking in other tongues.

Revival broke out in that church! The service went on through the night, with people dancing, singing, shouting, and rejoicing in the Lord.

The next day, my husband and I left to minister at another church. A few days later we received a call from the pastor of the Gypsy church.

He explained that the teens had been so on fire for God they had stayed overnight at the youth pastor's house. They were up until five in the morning praying in tongues. Later that morning they had a pancake breakfast and were planning to go swimming afterwards.

The youth pastor's wife told her husband she had a "bad feeling" about them going swimming; they shouldn't be allowed to go. He told her she was just worrying because they had been up all night. But again she mentioned they shouldn't go. She still had a very bad feeling about it.

The group went swimming as planned. That morning, the boy who had urgently requested the baptism of the Holy Spirit the night before, dove off a diving board, broke his neck and died.

The pastor of the church asked us to come back as soon as possible. The youth group was falling apart. They were angry, and unable to understand how they had just gotten saved and filled with the Holy Spirit and then had one of them suddenly die right in front of them.

We returned to their church to minister to the whole grieving congregation.

The boy's mother came to see me. For weeks before her son died, she'd had visions of him in a coffin.

"I didn't know what to do about it," she said. "I just thought I was having bad dreams."

Later I told the whole congregation how the Holy Spirit had been trying to send them warnings about what was going to happen. Satan, the enemy of our souls, sets traps for people. Jesus said that the devil **"does not come except to steal, and to kill, and to destroy."**

In contrast, Jesus said, **"I have come that they may have life, and that they may have it more abundantly"** (John10:10).

The Holy Spirit will warn you and show you when things are wrong. The Lord tried to warn that mother in visions. She should have told the pastor and gotten the whole church praying. Though the youth pastor's wife had been given guidance by the Holy Spirit, the urgency of her words wasn't recognized.

Clearly we need to always be built up in the Holy Spirit, and be sensitive to His leading. You never know when Satan will attempt to snuff you out, or kill a loved one or neighbor before your time. We can be prepared in the Lord. Had my son Rob died, he would have wound up in hell because he had not yet received Jesus as Lord. But the Lord saved him.

Thank God the young Gypsy boy got saved and filled with the Holy Spirit the day before he died, but his death was not for God's glory. That was the work of the devil. It was Satan who came to kill him, not God. The Holy Spirit gave warning, but no one had enough sensitivity to recognize His voice and heed His leading.

Our Heavenly Father wants all of us to be able to hear His voice and obey the leading of the Holy Spirit.

Stay built up in the Holy Spirit so that you can hear clearly!

Chapter 13

On the Count of One!

The early Church preached the Gospel through the Holy Spirit, who was sent from Heaven. God has anointed His people today with the same anointing He placed on the early Church. The same Holy Spirit is here with you and me today. We need to be able to preach the Gospel today under the anointing of the Holy Spirit.

> **To them it was revealed that, not to themselves, but to us they were ministering the things which now have been reported to you through those who have preached the gospel to you by the Holy Spirit sent from heaven — things which angels desire to look into.** (1Peter 1:12)

When we are preaching and sharing Jesus with others, the Holy Spirit will speak through us. The Holy Spirit knows the person to whom we are witnessing. He knows everything about everyone. God Himself will direct what needs to be said. When we speak what the Holy Spirit is saying, that Word is being spoken right into the person's heart. Their heart will hear, allowing them to receive Jesus as Lord.

God desires His people to be totally obedient to Him. As we learn to be obedient to the Holy Spirit, God can use us more and more to impact lives.

And we are His witnesses to these things, and so also is the Holy Spirit whom God has given to those who obey Him. (Acts 5:32)

When my daughter Carrie was young, she sometimes kept a very messy bedroom. Teenagers don't always keep their bedrooms as clean as they should, as some of you reading this may very well know. One day I went in there and told her she needed to get her room cleaned up. I gave her a time limit.

Twice I checked whether her room was clean or not, and it wasn't done. I told her if it wasn't done by the third time I checked, she'd be in trouble.

As I was walking back downstairs after my second check, I heard the Holy Spirit ask, "Does it upset you to have to tell your daughter something three times before she obeys you?"

"Well, yes, " I said. "It would be wonderful if she would just obey me on the count of one."

The Holy Spirit replied, "It would be really wonderful if you would obey Me when you hear Me, on the count of one."

I gasped aloud, "Wow, Lord!"

I said, "Holy Spirit, I want to be obedient on the count of one. I don't want you to have to tell me two and three times." Before that, I'd sometimes found myself, like most people, telling the Holy Spirit things like, "Lord, if that's really You speaking, then tell me again." Now I realized that you and I can know the voice of God, and we can begin being obedient to Him on the count of one.

What the Holy Spirit said caused me to pray differently. But when you pray for something you had better be ready to receive it!

The Lady in the Brown Dress

While preaching in Alaska that winter, the weather was very icy and cold. We didn't let that stop us from going out door-to-door evangelizing and sharing Jesus in the community. We'd just finished a week of revival meetings and the pastor wanted to take people out to witness. He and I were in his pick up truck driving up and down, praying and asking the Holy Ghost to show us the area where He wanted us to go door-to-door.

As we headed back towards the church we saw a woman in a brown dress walking away from a phone booth. As we drove past her, a strong spirit of compassion came upon me and I began weeping for her. Then I heard the Holy Spirit say, "Follow her; follow her!"

I immediately told the pastor to turn the truck around. I told him that though I didn't know her, the Lord wanted me to speak with that lady in the brown dress.

As he pulled over to the curb, we saw her enter an apartment complex. He stayed in the truck praying, while I followed her into the complex.

There were apartments on both sides, so by the time I entered the courtyard I'd lost her. I prayed, "Holy Spirit, I've lost the lady in the brown dress. You can either give me her address or have her come back outside so I can see where she is!"

Right away, I saw her come out of an apartment and head across towards another apartment. Not wanting to lose sight of her again, I ran across the courtyard, and followed her up a flight of stairs. By the time I got near her she was knocking on an apartment door.

A lady opened the door, and I followed the woman inside. I had no idea what the Holy Spirit was doing. I was just trying to be obedient on the count of one!

Once inside, I told them, "Excuse me, I know you don't know me, and I probably shouldn't have scared you like this. Please don't call the police on me!" They looked at me strangely, as I said to the lady in the brown dress, "I need to talk to you. God showed me that you just had a trauma."

I think the Lord had a lot more words of knowledge He was about to speak through me, but that was as far as I got because she began staring at me! Then she started screaming at the top of her voice, and ran off into one of the bedrooms. Still screaming and crying, she slammed the door.

The woman who lived there turned to me and said, "Look what you've done! You've upset my friend." She followed her friend into the bedroom, closing the door behind her.

I was left alone in the living room, thinking I'd better leave quickly, before they called the police. Yet I found I could not move; my feet were literally stuck to the floor. Realizing the Lord wasn't letting me leave right away, I stood there listening to the cries coming from the bedroom. They were just touching my heart. Figuring that the Lord had kept me there because of the lady in the brown dress, I decided to go into the bedroom to see how she was.

It's definitely not normal to walk into the home of a total stranger, much less go into one of their bedrooms. However I felt the Lord leading me to go in, hug this woman, and let her know everything would be all right.

As I began walking down the hall, the apartment owner was coming out of the bedroom and she asked me where I was going. "Look, I said, I just need to talk to that lady. Please, I'm not a bad person, it's just that God has something for me to tell her." She told me to go sit in the living room and she would get her. The woman with the brown dress came out and sat near me.

I knelt in front of her and said, "I didn't mean to frighten you, but the Lord told me that you've just had a terrible experience happen in your life." She said yes, it was true.

She told me she didn't have a phone and her friend helped get messages to her. She'd received a message to call Seattle right away, and had gone to the phone booth to call. They told her that her grandmother had just died. Her grandmother was the only mother she'd ever known.

The news had shattered her heart.

As she was walking away from that phone booth, she had asked God to give her a sign that her grandmother was now in Heaven with Him.

"That must have been the very moment we drove by," I said, "and the Lord told me I needed to talk to you."

She looked at me and said, "You must be the sign I asked God for. Now I know my grandma's in Heaven."

Looking into her eyes, I told her, "Isn't that wonderful that God would give you assurance to know that your grandmother's in Heaven?" She agreed. Then I asked, "What about you? Would you be in Heaven?"

She hung her head, and I knew from her posture that she did not know Jesus as Lord. I looked up at the other lady and asked her the same thing. She hung her head as well. I wanted to tell them both about Jesus right away.

The Holy Spirit said, "No, I don't want you to talk to them right now. You've said enough, and you can leave now, Joan."

As I was leaving, I reached into my pocket and found my hotel key. The hotel's phone number was on the key ring, so I asked the Holy Spirit in my heart, if it was all right to give them my number, and he said yes.

I told the woman I'd be praying for her. She thanked me and said she would be flying out first thing the next morning to make the funeral arrangements.

I went back and explained to the pastor what had happened. Those women did not know I was a minister, they probably thought I was somebody off the street. Nevertheless, when I preached that night I had the whole church pray for them.

The next morning I sat in my room crying out to God to save them. I told Him, "I want that woman saved! I ask You to comfort her at the funeral! Oh God, please have them call me." No sooner had I finished praying than the phone rang.

The woman whose apartment I'd visited invited me over. She said she had a lot of questions. I thought, "Oh praise God!" I made arrangements to have the pastor accompany me there later that afternoon.

After we'd all sat down together, I asked her what she had on her heart. She told us it had to have been God who sent me the day before. When I left, she'd spent hours calling and telling everyone she knew what had happened with me and with her friend.

Then she went on to say that when she was fifteen she'd had a Baptist boyfriend who had told her that she needed to be "born again." Though he said she had to receive Jesus, she hadn't done anything about it then.

Now she told us that she'd decided her spirit wasn't quite right. She felt she needed to get born again. She asked if we knew how to do it.

"Wow," I thought, "this is so simple, Lord!"

We went over some scriptures together, and after about ten or fifteen minutes of sharing she prayed and asked Jesus into her heart.

That was the easy part.

When we'd finished praying, she shared something very disturbing. She said she was afraid. She had an infant son, asleep in the other room. She told us she was being tormented by a voice speaking into her mind, constantly telling her, "Kill your son. Kill your son."

When she went into his room to change his diaper or give him a bottle, she would often get sudden urges to put a pillow over his head and smother him. Sometimes she would get the urge to put her hands around his throat and choke him. She genuinely did not want to hurt her son. She didn't know where the voices were coming from.

We prayed deliverance over her, commanding the demon spirit that was tormenting her to leave her alone. That day she was set free. Praise God!

Afterwards, we led her into the baptism of the Holy Spirit, where she was wonderfully filled with God's presence and power.

Later on she contacted me and testified she was never again bothered by the voices, or by thoughts of killing her child. Her life was truly changed.

I learned the important lesson of being obedient to the voice of the Holy Spirit on the count of one.

As you pray to be obedient on the count of one, you will find yourself talking to people about Jesus without even thinking twice about it. You will just do it! That's what I wanted, to be obedient and allow God to use me. I wanted to be yielded to Him, so that whenever He spoke, I would be attentive to His voice.

Our prayer for you is that you will learn to hear clearly and recognize God's voice. When you hear His voice, simply obey it. The fact is that someone's life may be in danger.

Pray: God, teach me to clearly hear You, and to always be obedient to the voice of Your Holy Spirit on the Count of One.

Chapter 14

A Compassionate Heart

Then Jesus went about all the cities and villages, teaching in their synagogues, preaching the gospel of the kingdom, and healing every sickness and every disease among the people. But when He saw the multitudes, He was moved with compassion for them, because they were weary and scattered, like sheep having no shepherd. Then He said to His disciples, "The harvest is truly plentiful, but the laborers are few. Therefore pray the Lord of the harvest to send out laborers into His harvest."

(Matthew 9:35-38)

Jesus saw the multitudes. It is possible for us to go through our daily lives and not see the multitudes. "Multitudes" can be the next-door neighbor, the one down the street, the one at the supermarket, or the one at the gas station. Everywhere we go there are people who need to know Jesus. But do we see them?

Very early on in ministry I began praying every morning asking the Father to give me new eyes. I prayed my eyes would be sensitive enough to see through the eyes of Jesus.

As I made that my daily prayer, asking the Father to give me His heart for the lost, I no longer saw people the same way. The lady checking out my groceries in the supermarket was no longer just another lady, but rather she was an opportunity. She was someone I could tell about Jesus. Now I saw people and just wanted to reach out to them.

Scripture points out the steps. First we are to see the need. Second, we are to be like Jesus and be moved with compassion.

Compassion is something that touches the heart. Have you ever seen someone on the street holding a sign saying, "Will work for food," or an elderly woman carrying heavy bags of groceries on a hot day, and had your heart just go out to them? Perhaps your heart said, "Oh that poor person, they need help!"

To have compassion without taking action is to only have pity. True compassion means that in some way you act upon what you see. Jesus was moved with compassion. The word "moved" means changing position, taking a step, or doing something. When we see a hurting person, or someone without food, we need to reach out to them. We have to do what we can to help them.

The Lady with the Bag of Groceries

Some time ago, when I had my own business, I was driving to work. Out of the corner of my eye I saw a woman carrying a huge grocery bag. She was trying to lift it, but it kept slipping down. I happened to be stopped at a light. The temperature outside my air-conditioned car was about a hundred degrees. As I sat in my cool comfortable car watching this woman with sweat dripping down her face, with her hair all wet, I felt my heart go out to her.

I wondered where she was going with that bag. I pulled over and asked her if she wanted a ride.

"Well, I'm not sure," she said, "I don't know you."

"Well, I'm a Christian who loves Jesus and I won't hurt you. Please, get in the car out of the heat and I'll take you where you need to go," I said.

When she agreed, I helped her get in the car with her bag. She said she wanted to get to the grocery store six blocks up the street. As we drove, I asked her what was in the bag. She said it was a twenty-five pound bag of dog food. Then I asked her why she was returning it.

She explained that her husband got angry with her for buying dog food when they didn't have enough food in the house for themselves. She was now returning the dog food and was planning to use her refund to buy other groceries.

Clearly she needed food. How could I shut my heart of compassion and do nothing to help her? When I asked the Holy Spirit what He wanted me to do, He said, "Take her in and buy her some groceries."

I told her to keep the dog food, that she didn't have to return it. I would take her shopping.

She said, "But you don't even know me."

"That's right," I told her, "but God knows you and loves you."

We bought her enough groceries to stock her up really well. As we went through the store, I remembered what it was like to be poor, hungry and without food in my home. As we shopped together, I was able to share Jesus with her. By the time we got back to her house she had received the Lord and was saved!

I asked if I could go in to talk to her husband about Jesus. She said he would get really angry and be embarrassed because of the groceries. I said it was okay if I didn't talk with him just then, and put a Bible tract into one of the bags. I told her that when he calmed down later on, she could tell him what happened. Then she could have him read the tract or read it to him.

My compassion for this woman in such clear need, caused me to go the extra mile. Jesus was moved with compassion; He is our example. If you do nothing about what you see, then it's just having pity, or being caloused. Christians must put actions to the needs we see.

The next thing we have to do, according to the Scriptures, is pray that God will send forth more laborers. The harvest of souls in the world really is plentiful, and very ripe for the picking.

Men on the Freight Train

When I was in Monterey, California to minister, I

got up early one morning and drove down by the pier. As I was praying, I saw a freight train arrive. Two men jumped off the train and sat down on the beach. I felt sorry for them and my compassion kicked in.

I asked the Lord what He wanted me to do. He said, "I want them to have breakfast."

I drove down a few blocks to the nearest McDonald's, went through the drive-through window and got a couple of sacks of food. I quickly returned to the beach and walked over to the men.

"Hi guys," I said, "how ya' doing? I saw you jump off the freight train a little while ago, and God said He wants you to have breakfast. So here's your breakfast!"

I handed them the sacks of food. Then I said, "But before you eat, don't you think we should pray and bless the food?"

When they said yes, I said, "After all the breakfast is on God; He's the One who supplied your coffee and eggs this morning. Before you eat I'd like to take a few minutes to read some Scriptures to you." I read to them from a little tract I had in my hand.

Afterwards, I asked them if they wanted to pray and ask Jesus into their hearts right then before eating. They said they wanted to, and both of them prayed asking Jesus to be their Lord.

I wrote down their names. They had no addresses. How can you follow up when there is no address? People who are constantly going from place to place, or train to train, aren't likely to get involved in any local church. If you're ever in a situation where follow up with a newly saved person will be difficult or impossible, you can always simply jot down a person's name. Even if they don't choose to give you their real name, the name they give is an identifier, and a reminder for you to keep them lifted up in prayer.

I often keep the names of individuals in the front of my Bible. The Lord keeps me praying for them. You can keep a list as part of your daily devotions, praying for the ones you've led to the Lord. That is putting action to what the Lord tells us to do!

 **So keep a compassionate heart!**

Chapter 15

Street Rat

Here is a wonderful illustration showing how God used an elderly man who was filled with the love of Jesus to reach the lost.

> One day the Holy Spirit told me to pick up a fifteen year-old boy who was hitchhiking. This is something I'd never recommend new Christians do, as it is generally unwise and could be dangerous. I only did it in this instance because I was sure the Holy Spirit had spoken to me to do it.
>
> I had stopped at a rest area on my way to Salt Lake City to do a revival. As I was pulling back out onto the highway, the Holy Spirit spoke to me. "Just ahead a few miles, you'll see a young man standing near the highway. I want you to pick him up." Telling me ahead of time was God's way of preparing me, so I'd be ready to step out and do something I'd never have done otherwise.
>
> Just as I'd been told, three miles down the road I came up on a teenager wearing a leather jacket. He looked like a pretty rough character. But the Lord said, "That's him. Pick him up."
>
> I pulled over, and he got in the car. He said he was going to Georgia. I told him I could take him as far as

Salt Lake City. As we talked, the Holy Spirit told me he had been hitchhiking all day, and was hungry. Not wanting to embarrass him, I said I was hungry and wanted to stop to eat, and I would treat him. He ate a really good lunch!

As we ate he began explaining about his trip to Georgia. When he was thirteen years old, his mom had suddenly left him and his dad, and disappeared. His dad had tried very hard to raise him, but one day he returned home from school to an empty house. There was no furniture, only his clothes, packed in the middle of the living room floor.

Unsure of what to do, he had waited there a few days, thinking his father would return. When he didn't and the food ran out, the boy realized he was on his own. He then started hitchhiking, and wound up in Portland, Oregon.

There he became what he referred to as a "street rat." He explained that the group he joined up with called themselves the "street rat pack." He was the oldest of this group of ten or fifteen children, some as young as seven or eight. They were living in a park in Portland.

When I asked him how they survived, he explained their system for getting food. When the fast food and donut shops closed for the night, they always threw their leftovers in a dumpster. When the children were sure no one was around, they jumped the fence took food out of the garbage. They took baths at the city pools.

He told me it was scary being on the streets. They slept during the day, and prowled around for food at night when no one could see them.

Then he explained how he'd been able to locate his father. He said there was a man who had started coming to the park to help the children. The man was a Christian, and had talked to them all the time about Jesus. For the most part, they really didn't want to hear about God. They had been hurt pretty badly and they didn't believe there was a big, good God who was doing things to help people. They couldn't relate to there being a God who loved them. They were stuck on the streets, alone, freezing and hungry all the time.

Still the man kept telling them about Jesus. "He kept on, even when we didn't care about living forever. Why would we want to live forever when we were having hell on earth?"

"One night he came to the park with blankets and sleeping bags. He left them and said they were there for whenever we wanted them. A couple of days later he left plates and plates of spaghetti. He then began leaving coats, gifts, and all kinds of stuff. He even told us that if we let him know our shoe sizes he would get us all new sneakers."

Slowly but surely the younger ones in the group began going up to him. Then he started taking them to his home. The young man said that since he was considered the pack leader, he held out until he was the only one left there. It got so cold that he finally agreed to go with the man, but only for a couple of days. He planned on returning to the park. When he arrived there, everyone was sleeping in sleeping bags.

"He kept telling me about Jesus and it finally got through this hard head of mine. About four months ago I asked Jesus into my heart to be my Lord and Savior."

The teen said the man had taken them all in at his own expense. He wasn't getting help from anyone. He fed them and loved them, teaching them the Bible every day, being a father to them. Because of him, they weren't on the streets cold and starving anymore.

"Finally," he said, "the man even called around to some of my relatives to see if anyone knew what had happened to my dad."

"Guess what happened." he continued, "When I finally got in contact with dad, God had been working on the other end! My dad had also received Jesus into his heart, but didn't know how to find me! That man from the park got us connected! There wasn't any money for them to put me on a train or plane, so that's why I'm hitchhiking."

I asked him if the man had taught him about the baptism of the Holy Spirit. He said he hadn't, and asked me what it was all about. During the rest of our long drive I had plenty of time to share with him. At one of the rest stops he prayed and received the baptism of the Holy Spirit. After that he went on to be with his dad in Georgia.

That's what it's all about! One helps in one way, and another helps in another way, but we are part of the family of God. God Himself is Love and that's why we must reach out in love. If we are to be like God, then we must minister in love.

If you find yourself lacking the love of God in your heart, simply pray, "God, give me a loving heart. Lord Jesus, let me see the world through Your eyes. Change my heart so that my heart will be full of love. Make me a vessel of Your love."

The world will know that we are Christians by the love we demonstrate, not by our great preaching. They will know we are Christians by the love of God they see in us. God is Supreme Love. We, who are made in His image, are to be like Him.

> **"So God created man in His own image, in the image of God He created him; male and female He created them."** (Genesis 1:27)

It is God who has **"blessed us with every spiritual blessing in the heavenly places in Christ..."** (Ephesians 1:3). We who have been so greatly blessed are now called to go out into this lost and dying world to share that same love with others. There are hurting people everywhere who need to know about the love of God.

My husband and I enjoy cooking a lot of food while we're traveling. We usually stay in campgrounds along the way. Marty often wraps some food in foil and we bring it over to share with other campers. Sometimes he even ties a bow around the plate.

We'll go up to total strangers and say, "Hi! We'd like to bless you." It's a great tool to open possibilities to share about Jesus. Sometimes you have to build a friendship before you can share.

We are to love people even if they never come to the Lord. However, the goal of our hearts should always be to see souls get saved. Truly loving people means not wanting anyone to miss going to Heaven. That's the cry of our Heavenly Father's heart, and that's the cry of our hearts.

 **Let God's love lead you to hurting people.**

Chapter 16

Manifestations of the Holy Spirit

Love and compassion are the keys that unlock the door to the operations and manifestations of the Holy Spirit. God has given many spiritual gifts, and made them available to His children. He wants us to know about them and desire to have them. Throughout a lengthy discussion of the spiritual gifts in 1Corinthians, chapters 12 to 14, Paul emphasizes love as the essential element. If we fully operate in all of the gifts of the Holy Spirit and lack love we are useless.

As Paul put it:

"And though I... understand all mysteries and all knowledge, and though I have all faith, so that I could remove mountains, but have not love, I am nothing." (1Corinthians13:2)

He went on to say:

Pursue love, and desire spiritual gifts, but especially that you may prophesy. For he who speaks in a tongue does not speak to men but to God, for no one understands him; however, in the spirit he speaks mysteries. But he who prophesies speaks edification and exhortation and comfort to men. He who speaks in a tongue edifies himself, but he who prophesies edifies

the church. I wish you all spoke with tongues, but even more that you prophesied; for he who prophesies is greater than he who speaks with tongues, unless indeed he interprets, that the church may receive edification.

(1Corinthians 14:1-5)

Notice the order of Paul's instructions: first, "pursue love," and then, "desire spiritual gifts." All of us who genuinely desire to have the manifestations of the Holy Spirit operate in our lives need to confront our heart motivation. Do we want the Holy Spirit operating in our life so that we can be noticed and impress others? Clearly that is a wrong heart motive. The right heart motive for having the Holy Spirit use us is to see people's lives changed. We want to see others healed, saved, delivered and comforted by the love and grace of the Lord Jesus.

Therefore I make known to you that no one speaking by the Spirit of God calls Jesus accursed, and no one can say Jesus is Lord except by the Holy Spirit. (1Corinthians 12:3)

No one can come to Jesus, inviting Him into their heart, unless the Holy Spirit is drawing them. We know that the Holy Spirit is drawing people to salvation. The most important key is that no one can be saved without the Holy Spirit, because the wind blows where the Lord sends it out. When we lift Jesus up, sharing Him with someone, the Holy Spirit takes what we share and explains it to them, or has them keep hearing it. God will take our efforts and the Holy Spirit will enhance them until the individual comes to the saving knowledge of Jesus Christ.

The gifts and manifestations of the Holy Spirit are actually tools God has provided for us to do the work of harvesting souls. A farmer needs the right tools to till the ground. A doctor needs the correct supplies and medicines to treat patients. God has tools for us to do Kingdom business for Him.

> **There are diversities of gifts, but the same Spirit. There are differences of ministries, but the same Lord. And there are diversities of activities, but it is the same God who works all in all.**
>
> **But the manifestation of the Spirit is given to each one for the profit of all: for to one is given the word of wisdom through the Spirit, to another the word of knowledge through the same Spirit, to another faith by the same Spirit, to another gifts of healings by the same Spirit, to another working of miracles, to another prophecy, to another discerning of spirits, to another different kinds of tongues, to another the interpretation of tongues.**
>
> **But one and the same Spirit works all these things, distributing to each one individually as He wills.** (1Corinthians 12:4-11)

No one "owns" the Holy Spirit. The Holy Spirit will use you according to God's desire. The gifts do not belong to you. But everything is available to you when you yield yourself by accepting Jesus as your Lord and Savior and then inviting the Holy Spirit to come and live inside of you.

The Bible says:

"Or do you not know that your body is the temple of the Holy Spirit who is in you, whom you have from God, and you are not your own?"

(1Corinthians 6:19)

With the Holy Spirit living inside you, you are actually "on call" twenty-four hours a day. When you witness to people, you never know which of the gifts the Holy Spirit will manifest for you to use with a particular person. It might be a word of wisdom for clarity in their lives. It may be a miracle of healing. When they get healed they will say, "Wow! God is real! I just received a miracle!" When we are yielded to God, He will manifest His anointing through us.

A life can be changed and transformed because God will use us. The Holy Spirit who dwells in us is God Himself. He is not an "it" or a "thing." The Holy Spirit is the Third Person of the Godhead. We have the Father, Son and Holy Spirit working in us.

In yielding ourselves to the operations and manifestations of the Spirit, we will walk in the miraculous. These are not our miracles, but God's miracles! Remember that the key to moving in the gifts of the Spirit is love. Jesus said:

> **"Not everyone who says to Me, 'Lord, Lord,' shall enter the kingdom of heaven, but he who does the will of My Father in heaven. Many will say to Me in that day, 'Lord, Lord, have we not prophesied in Your name, cast out demons in Your name and done many wonders in Your name?' And then I will declare to them, 'I never knew you; depart from Me, you who practice lawlessness!'"**
>
> (Matthew 7:21-23)

You can be doing great things, even thinking you know Jesus, but if your heart motive isn't pure, you will be in big trouble! There are some people today who want to move in the gifts of the Holy Spirit so that they can be noticed or recognized. This is a wrong motive!

There is truly one motive for wanting to let the Holy Spirit use you, and that is so lives can be changed. Our first desire must be for love, and then the desire for spiritual gifts. Someone who only desires the spiritual gifts, but doesn't have love, can be cruel to others. They may see something in the realm of the Spirit concerning a person, and then go and reveal all this person's problems, embarrassing them. God's way is to be polite, kind and courteous to people at all times.

What's So Funny?

We were out ministering with a church one day, going door to door. We had some people with us, but we weren't getting anywhere from knocking on doors. Not much was happening. I had told my group we needed to pray some more and let the Lord lead us, then we would be more in tune with what God would have us do. We joined hands there on the sidewalk and began praying in the Holy Ghost: "Oh Holy Spirit lead and guide us. Show us what Your will is. Show us where You want us to go Lord."

The Lord answered us. He said, "See down the road there? Go knock on the door of that house with the white picket fence." So we walked down and knocked on the door.

When a man came and opened it, we said, "Hi, we're Christians and we're in the neighborhood. We're not trying to promote a church or anything. We're just asking people to help us fill out a questionnaire so we can find out how Christians can be more helpful in this area. There may be people here who need clothing, food or other kinds of help. Can we come in for a few minutes and just ask a few questions?"

He said, "Oh yes, sure. Come on in." We sat down in the living room, with him and his two sons.

We began going through the questionnaire, talking to him about the Lord. I got down to the last two questions and asked, "If you were to die tonight, would you know beyond a shadow of a doubt that you would be in heaven?"

Now that's a pretty serious question, but he and his two boys started laughing out loud. They were laughing hysterically.

The father said, "We're not trying to be rude, but we couldn't help laughing." He turned to one of the boys and said, "Son, tell her what you asked me before they came to the door."

The boy, who was about ten, told us he'd just asked his dad, "Where would we go if we were to die?" Right after that we knocked on the door. It struck them as funny that we were asking the same question they'd just asked.

"We don't really know where we would go," he said.

"Well we can share with you how you can know where you would go."

We shared God's plan of salvation, telling them they needed to have their spirits born again, and invite Jesus into their hearts to be Lord. A few minutes later they all received Jesus into their hearts. When the father and his two sons finished praying I asked if anyone else lived in the home. He said he had a wife and two teenage daughters who were out shopping.

Since the man is the spiritual head of the household, I instructed him that he had the responsibility to make sure his family was saved. He was to teach them the Word of God and show them the plan of salvation if they were not saved.

I told him, "You and your sons are now saved and will go to Heaven. You wouldn't want to be in Heaven without your wife and daughters, would you?" "No, I wouldn't," he said.

I said, "As the high priest of your home and family, it's your responsibility to make sure your family is saved." I asked if we could set a time to come back to do a Bible study with his family. He agreed to have a meeting on Friday at 7:00 p.m.

When you lead someone to the Lord, you should always try to find out who their friends and relatives are, so they can be saved too.

I had to leave to go to another revival meeting, so I wasn't there for the Bible study. However, a few weeks later the pastor contacted me. "Sister Joan," he said, "what in the world did you say to that Spanish man? When we went to do the Friday night study, there must have been twenty-five people in the house."

Apparently he'd invited all his aunts, uncles and cousins to a 6:00 enchilada dinner. He told them it was urgent that they come, because he had something very important to share with the whole family.

Clearly this man took literally the responsibility for seeing that his whole extended family were saved. He didn't just think about his wife and daughters. That night his entire family prayed and invited Jesus to be their Lord and Savior.

It was the manifestation of the gifts of the Holy Spirit that led us to that house. God had already prepared them. That's why it's so important to be sensitive to the Holy Spirit's leading. The gifts of the Spirit are powerful tools to be used of God. But earnestly desire the best gift.

> **...And yet I show you a more excellent way. Though I speak with the tongues of men and of angels, but have not love, I have become sounding brass or a clanging cymbal. And though I have the gift of prophecy, and understand all mysteries and all knowledge, and though I have all faith, so that I could remove mountains, but have not love, I am nothing. And though I bestow all my goods to feed the poor, and though I give my body to be burned, but have not love, it profits me nothing.** (1Corinthians 12:31-13:3)

The Apostle Paul pointed out that the greatest gift one can desire is love. Begin now to pray to God:

> *Lord make me a vessel of Your love. Holy Spirit, let me be yielded to You as a vessel who no longer lives for myself, but Christ lives in and through me. I just want to yield myself to You, that Your will be done.*

Now that you have prayed for God to use you, you will begin to walk in the gifts of the Spirit! It will simply start happening.

Love is the key to moving in the Gifts of the Holy Spirit.

Chapter 17

The Anointing

But you have an anointing from the Holy One, and you know all things. (1 John 2:20)

You have an anointing from the Holy One once the Holy Spirit is living inside of you! He will tell you which tool to use to help lead someone to Jesus. You won't have to worry about whether it's supposed to be a word of knowledge, a word of wisdom, a gift of miracles, or a prophecy. The Holy Spirit will supernaturally use you as you yield to Him.

This also means that you will have to trust the Lord. You need to know that when you are leading people to Jesus you are doing the work of God to advance His Kingdom. You have to trust God is going to take care of you. He will provide for you.

When we go out preaching the Gospel, we expect miracles to happen. When you're preaching the Gospel and lifting Jesus up to a world that is crying out, expect miracles!

I was doing a tent revival in Pendleton, Oregon with my husband Marty. He had a cousin who was in prison in that area. I was given the opportunity to preach at the prison. I preached to about forty "macho" men there. God got hold of them to the point that they had tears running down their faces, and they all received Jesus into their hearts. I taught about the baptism of the Holy Spirit, and they all came forward to be filled with the Holy Spirit.

As I laid hands on them, they began to fall under the power of God. Evidently one of the guards thought there was some kind of riot going on. He almost hit the alarm.

Thank God another guard saw what was happening and told him, "Stop! She's just praying for people." (I was then strongly advised to let them know before starting to pray for people again. That way any new guards would be prepared for what might occur after that!)

Expect A Miracle

While I was at the prison, Marty had spent hours talking with another of his cousins who lived in the area. I arrived home from the prison revival really exhausted. Soon Marty advised me that his cousin was a leader in a small Women's Aglow ministry that was going to be shut down because of very low attendance. He had told her that if the group could get on the phones through the night and invite people, telling them to expect miracles, he would send me to speak the next day!

Although I was looking forward to having a couple of days off, I got my friend Becky to take the four-hour drive with me. We prayed in the Holy Spirit throughout the whole ride.

The service was the following morning and they sure did invite a lot of people. Marty had told them all about the miracles which were happening in other meetings, and so they brought people who needed healing. Some were just out of the hospital, and came with portable oxygen tanks! They were told to come expecting the miraculous and that's just what they were doing. Some people had been up all night, praying, with excitement and anticipation of seeing the miracle working power of God.

God is still telling us today: "Expect a miracle! The Kingdom of God is at hand!" If Jesus had not had any miracles occurring, people would not have come out. The miracles drew them to Jesus. Then He could preach the Kingdom of God to them.

I began to pray for people at the meeting and they began to fall out under the power of God. It was because they were expecting Jesus. Jesus is the One who is the Miracle-Worker. We are simply vessels for the Holy Spirit to work through.

After the service they planned a small luncheon for us. We set up our book and tape table while we waited. A woman whom we had prayed for came over to us. Her leg was in a brace up to her ankle, because part of her foot had been removed.

She said, "Sister Joan, my foot is on fire!" I told her it was okay, that Jesus was healing her foot.

She came back again just before we went to lunch. "It's been forty-five minutes since you prayed for me and my foot still feels like it's on fire!" Again I reassured her that it was just the Lord healing her.

Nevertheless, after lunch she came by again to tell me her foot still felt like it was on fire.

Hours after I arrived back home, I had a message on my answering machine. It was the same woman. She said that several hours after being prayed over she removed the leg brace. Her foot was perfectly whole. All the flesh that had been removed due to disease was restored! God gave her a creative miracle!

God wants us all to expect miracles. People will get new eyes, new arteries, new limbs, whatever is needed! I believe there is a whole Throne Room full of body parts and all we have to do is call them down! It means walking by faith in the anointing of God, knowing that God Almighty is a miracle-working God. Expect miracles. The greatest miracle is someone coming to know Jesus as their Savior. God intends to use you and me today!

EXPECT MIRACLES!

Chapter 18

Miracles Bring People to Jesus

As you read the scriptures it's evident that it was the miracles that drew the multitudes to Jesus. They came to see and experience miracles and stayed to hear His message. Today the world is still looking for the miraculous. Miracles bring people to a place where they can meet Jesus.

> **"Do you not believe that I am in the Father, and the Father in Me? The words that I speak to you I do not speak of My own authority; but the Father who dwells in Me does the works.**
>
> **Believe Me that I am in the Father and the Father in Me, or else believe Me for the sake of the works themselves."** (John 14:10-11)

Jesus was speaking to His disciples that the Father was doing the miracles through Him. The evidence was what they actually saw: blind eyes opened, His feeding of the five thousand, and countless other miracles. When people see miracles, they believe and know that God is real indeed.

I remember a little church service somewhere in the mountains, where there was a great outpouring of the

Holy Spirit. During the service the Lord had me call up two little girls about six and seven years old. As I prayed, the power of God hit them. They were down on the floor shaking and quivering under the power of God. After the service, one of them told me, "Sister Joan, we've been in church all our lives, and now we know personally that Jesus is our Lord and Savior."

People are hungry. They are looking for miracles. As believers in Jesus Christ, we have the same power that raised Christ from the dead living inside of us!

> **"Most assuredly, I say to you, he who believes in Me, the works that I do he will do also; and greater works than these he will do, because I go to My Father. And whatever you ask in My name, that I will do, that the Father may be glorified in the Son.**
>
> **"If you ask anything in My name, I will do it. If you love Me, keep My commandments. And I will pray the Father, and He will give you another Helper that He may abide with you forever — the Spirit of truth, whom the world cannot receive, because it neither sees Him nor knows Him; but you know Him, for He dwells with you and will be in you. I will not leave you orphans; I will come to you."** (John 14:12-18)

Jesus was telling His disciples about the Baptism of the Holy Spirit. As He continued speaking with them,

He said:

> **"But the Helper, the Holy Spirit, whom the Father will send in My name, He will teach you all things, and bring to your remembrance all things that I said to you. Peace I leave with you, My peace I give to you; not as the world gives do I give to you. Let not your heart be troubled, neither let it be afraid."**
>
> (John 14:26-27)

You don't have to be afraid to pray for the sick. You don't need to be afraid to cast out devils, or even to raise the dead. You don't need to be afraid to pray for people with leprosy.

You do need to know that you are being used by the Father, the Son, and the Holy Spirit, and that the same power will flow through you. Remember this, when you pray: "In Jesus' Name."

God says to go lay hands on the sick and believe. Expect miracles to happen when you pray for people.

Three of the gospels, Matthew 9, Mark 5 and Luke 8, tell about a woman who was afflicted with an issue of blood for twelve years. She'd spent all her money on physicians, trying to be cured, but she was not healed. When she heard about Jesus, she declared in her heart that if she could just **"touch the hem of His garment,"** she would be healed. Against all odds, she pressed through a large crowd to touch the hem of Jesus' garment, and she was instantly healed by the power and virtue of Christ.

Issue of Blood

At a revival meeting, a woman told me about her friend who had been bleeding for three months straight. She'd already been to specialists who weren't able to diagnose the problem. Her friend was getting weaker; and the doctors couldn't help her. So this woman asked us to pray that she'd be able to get her sick friend to come to the revival meeting. She believed that God would heal her friend.

We prayed and believed God to get her to the meeting to receive her miracle. We were told the woman belonged to a church that did not believe that miracles are for today. Therefore she did not believe in prayer or the laying on of hands.

"We believe and we've prayed" I told her friend. "So we're just going to leave this in God's hands."

Sure enough, her friend came to the meeting. When I did the altar call for healing, about fifty people lined up for prayer. The Holy Spirit directed me to have "catchers" in place and to "be ready".

I sensed in my spirit that there was a "wave of God" coming and I suddenly said, "Catchers be ready!" I told all the people who had their hands lifted up to "Just touch Jesus! Jesus is your Healer. Put up your hands, close your eyes, and just touch Jesus!

He will heal you!"

Bang! They started falling without anyone touching them or laying hands on them.

In the prayer line was the woman with the issue of blood. She went down when the wave of God hit her. No one was standing near her. She could never say someone pushed her down.

When she got up, guess what? The blood flow had stopped. Whatever was causing it was gone instantly. She never experienced it again.

The doctors couldn't heal her, but Jesus, the Great Physician, could!

The Bible says that **"Jesus Christ is the same yesterday, today, and forever"** (Hebrews 13:8).

We just need to believe and then reach out and touch Jesus. The miracle was done two thousand years ago when Jesus went to the cross at Calvary. Jesus has already taken our sicknesses, diseases, sins, sorrows and grief. Jesus took upon His body all our pains. And because Jesus did this, all we have to do is acknowledge it and receive it. Jesus has paid the price for us in full!

Beloved, if you desire to allow the Holy Spirit to use you to bless others, you can expect miracles. Remember what Jesus said:

> **"Most assuredly, I say to you, he who believes in Me, the works that I do he will do also; and greater works than these he will do, be-**

cause I go to My Father. And whatever you ask in My name, that I will do, that the Father may be glorified in the Son. (John 14:12-13)

Step out and pray for the sick "In Jesus' Name."

God has given us authority in the name of Jesus to go forth into the highways and byways to preach the Kingdom of God: to raise the dead, heal the sick, cleanse the lepers — to preach the Gospel.

It is God's heart for us to go and preach the Gospel. Don't worry about finances or other details. Just do what the scripture says:

But seek first the kingdom of God, and His righteousness, and all these things shall be added to you. (Matthew 6:33)

God will take care of us all the days of our lives and God will take care of you, too!

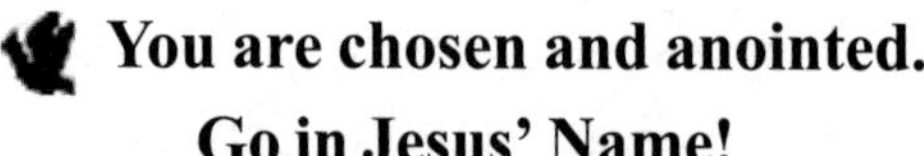

You are chosen and anointed.
Go in Jesus' Name!

Chapter 19

God Does the Miraculous

When we are committed to hearing God and obeying Him, we can walk in the miraculous. When we actually care more about someone else's need for healing or deliverance than for our own needs, God does the miraculous. It's a matter of not being affected by what we are seeing or feeling at the time.

I learned this especially from what happened with a woman who came to a summer tent revival meeting we held several years ago.

Woman in a Wheelchair

One day during the meetings my husband Marty said, "Why don't you start believing for people to come out of wheelchairs." I agreed with him. So we prayed that God would start bringing people in wheelchairs to our meetings.

At our first morning service the following week, a woman in a wheelchair rolled up to the front. I prayed for her with all my heart. Yet she rolled back to where she had come from. We wanted so much to see her come out of the wheelchair. Our hearts were breaking when we saw nothing had happening. She attended both the morning and evening services that first day.

The second day, she came back and rolled up to the front again. When we prayed for the sick, there were people lying on the floor everywhere, who had fallen out under the power of the Holy Spirit. She sat in her wheelchair in the midst of them.

She came back on the third night. Again the presence of God touched people. Some were on the floor, some were laughing, jumping, singing and shouting. She had rolled up to the front again, and wound up in the middle of all those lying on the floor. She couldn't move the wheelchair anywhere without running over the bodies, so she was kind of stuck in that place.

The service seemed to be coming to a close that night. We were singing praise songs when Marty suddenly came over and whispered in my ear. "Honey, you see that lady over there in the wheelchair?" I said, "Yes," and he said, "Look at her. She's so happy for everyone else who's being healed! She's sitting there with joy all over her face as she's seeing the people on the floor shaking under the power of the Anointing. She's watching God move in their lives. She's not even thinking about herself in that wheelchair. She's simply enjoying everyone else being blessed by God. I believe the Lord wants you to pray for her now!"

I made my way over to her, took her hand and started praying for her. There was no eloquent prayer. The truth is, I couldn't get a word to come out, not even one. Yet in my heart I kept repeating, "Jesus. Jesus. Jesus."

Suddenly Marty came over. He bent down and lifted the two footrests out of the way. The woman stood up. She just stood up!

She said to me, "Let's walk." She took three or four steps holding my hand. Remember the floor was still covered with those who had fallen under the power of the Holy Spirit.

Then she let go of my hand and took off dancing. Without ever stepping on anyone, she spun and stepped around the tent. When she stopped dancing she began weeping and crying. Then she paused and knelt down before a young girl who was in a wheelchair and began to pray for her.

We learned this woman had been afflicted with hepatitis C. The disease had progressed to a point where she could no longer walk, due to lack of strength in her legs. She had been receiving treatments at the University of Berkeley Hospital in California. Doctors had told her she would die soon if she did not get a new liver.

I simply prayed what God placed on my heart for her, saying, "God give her a creative miracle."

Thursday of that week, she returned to the hospital for scheduled tests. After they'd completed their tests, the doctor told her, "We don't know what's happened to you, but somehow you have a brand new liver!"

Before she came out of that wheelchair, the woman attended four services and was prayed for at each one. The point is, she heard God tell her "Keep on going," and so she kept on attending services. When God decided it was time, He just pulled her up out of that chair.

She could easily have become discouraged after the first service when we prayed and there were no apparent results. She could have become discouraged the next day and not returned for the other services. But she determined that if she kept coming, God would lift her up and out of that chair. And He did!

I tell you the day is approaching when we will see everybody getting up out of wheelchairs and walking. But this will require not only being ready, willing, and able to hear the voice of the Holy Spirit, but also ready to obey His voice when He speaks.

We need to know the voice of God's Holy Spirit, because we are clearly heading into difficult times in this world. God Almighty has given us a mandate from Heaven. He has told us, "Teach My people how to hear My voice, and how to listen and obey the Holy Spirit's voice."

God says His people hear His Voice, and the voice of a stranger they will not follow.

Chapter 20

You are Chosen and Anointed

To say you are chosen and anointed means that someone outside of you has made a decision about you and done something about it. The one who made the decision to choose and anoint you is God. Isn't it wonderful that Jesus said:

> **"You did not choose Me, but I chose you and appointed you that you should go and bear fruit, and that your fruit should remain, that whatever you ask the Father in My name He may give you. These things I command you, that you love one another."** (John 15:16-17)

When you walk in the gifts, when you walk in love and the fruit of the Spirit, you will walk in the manifestations of the Holy Spirit, lifting up Jesus everywhere you go. You will be a fruit bearer.

Notice that Jesus is saying we have not chosen Him, but He has chosen us. Many people think they choose to follow Jesus. We do finally yield to Him, when we say: "Dear Jesus come into my heart and be my Lord and Savior."

But the truth is that Jesus was always coming after us. We choose to do our own thing, often for a long time. But the Lord always pursues us. And one of the ways he pursues us is by having others witness to us. God has people pray for others to get saved. It is really about God choosing us!

Not only has God chosen us, but He has also anointed and ordained us, to use us for ministry. God wants you to know that He has placed an anointing on you to do miraculous things.

When Jesus died on the cross, the disciples scattered every which way. When He rose from the dead, He visited them.

> **Later He appeared to the eleven as they sat at the table; and He rebuked their unbelief and hardness of heart, because they did not believe those who had seen Him after he had risen.**
>
> **And He said to them, "Go into the all the world and preach the Gospel to every creature. He who believes and is baptized will be saved; but he who does not believe will be condemned.**
>
> **"And these signs will follow those who believe: In My name they will cast out demons; they will speak with new tongues; they will take up serpents; and if they drink anything deadly, it will by no means hurt them; they will lay hands on the sick, and they will recover."**
>
> **So then, after the Lord had spoken to them, He was received up into Heaven, and sat down at the right hand of God.**

> **And they went out and preached everywhere, the Lord working with them and confirming the word through the accompanying signs. Amen.** (Mark 16:14-20)

Isn't that wonderful? The word of God is so powerful. As we preach the Word, Jesus sets all of this into motion. As we obey the Word, by laying hands on the sick and casting out devils, people are healed and delivered. Lives are changed. God wants to use each of us to bring the miraculous into people's lives.

While I was working with a pastor in New York, we took some people from his congregation out witnessing in a tough neighborhood of the city of Newburgh. Before going out, I had instructed them to "Just be led by the Holy Spirit."

A young couple was with us, who'd only been saved for about two months. They stood out on the street corner holding hands, saying, "Sister Joan told us to pray in the Holy Ghost and He will tell us where to go."

Then the husband asked his wife, "Did you get anything?"

She asked him, "Did you?"

"No." he said. "We better just pray some more in the Holy Spirit."

After being there praying for about fifteen minutes, suddenly the husband said, "I hear a voice! It sounds like someone is saying, 'Come help me.' It sounds like it's coming from that apartment building over there."

They stopped and prayed on the first floor of the building, but didn't get anything. They walked up to the second floor and the third floors, still praying. When they got to the fourth floor, they heard the Holy Spirit say, "Knock on that door." When they knocked, they heard a faint voice say, "Come in; come in."

They opened the door, looked across the apartment, and saw a frail little lady. She said, "Oh, come help me; I've been crying out for help for hours."

She told them she had Lupus disease, and had been on the sofa in pain, unable to move.

Four stories down on the street there was no way anyone could have heard her cries for help. The husband heard and discerned her cries in the Holy Spirit. Isn't that wonderful!

They were two new Christians, but they told this woman, "We don't know many Scriptures, but we know this one in Mark, chapter 16. It says, **"...they will lay hands on the sick, and they will recover."**

The husband told her, "I'm a believer, and my wife is a believer, so when we lay hands on you, Jesus will heal you. You will get well. You've got Lupus disease and can't move. We believe what the Bible says, and so we're going to just close our eyes and do what this word says. We're going to lay our hands on you and pray."

They laid their hands on the crippled woman, praying, "Oh Jesus, you said in your Word that if we lay hands on the sick they will recover. So we say, 'In Jesus' name be healed!' We rebuke Lupus disease in this body!

Be healed in the name of Jesus!"

The lady jumped up, crying out, "The pain is gone! The pain is gone!" She jumped up and down all over her apartment. She told them, "This is awesome! " She said. "All of my joints were hurting and I couldn't move. It worked! It's Jesus!"

The couple told her there was another Scripture they knew, John 3:16:

> **"For God so loved the world that He gave His only begotten Son, that whoever believes in Him should not perish but have everlasting life."**

They explained that she needed to ask Jesus into her heart to be her Lord and Savior, and she agreed. They brought her the Word and she received Jesus. She had been unable to move, and crying for hours, then God sent them to her for her miracle.

They were so excited when they got back to the church. They came to me saying, "Sister Joan! God used us! We prayed for this lady and she was healed of Lupus disease! Then we led her to Jesus! We heard the Holy Spirit speaking to us!" God's promise to us is that if we believe, the signs will follow us!

We expect miracles at all of our revival meetings. We don't just have regular church services, we have revivals! We pray, "God Almighty, we ask You for an open Heaven. We ask You to visit us, Father, and do things that have never even been done before!" My husband is always saying we need to pray and believe for people to come out of wheelchairs, for limbs to grow out, and for the dead to be raised.

> **But as it is written:** ***"Eye has not seen, nor ear heard, nor have entered into the heart of man the things which God has prepared for those who love Him."*** (1Corinthians 2:9)

Notice the Scripture says, **"Eye has not seen."** Eyes have seen some pretty amazing things in the past. Ministers of the Gospel such as Aimee Semple McPherson, Kathryn Kuhlman, Smith Wigglesworth, and John G. Lake had awesome miracle services, where even the dead were raised. Yet God says there is yet more to come. We are going to experience things that we haven't even seen or heard about.

People like Mary Woodworth-Etter and Charles Finney saw whole areas come to Jesus through their preaching. When they prayed and preached, entire cities became convicted under the power of God. People began weeping and crying, and were saved. Still the Lord is telling us that we haven't seen anything yet! It's only going to get more awesome. The key is being so in love with God and allowing Him to use us through the power of His Holy Spirit. Then the anointing will flow.

For years we have seen miracles happen at our revival meetings across the nation. I've shared some of what we've seen and experienced in this book. We always press in and cry out to God for more. Here is another miracle we saw Jesus do.

The Twister

We were doing services night after night and miracles were happening. People were getting saved, and the power of God was getting stronger and stronger as each day progressed. While I prayed for the sick, my husband helped with getting people into the prayer line.

On the last night of the revival, I prayed for a little eight year old girl who came in. She was totally bald and wore a mask over her face. When I laid hands on her, the power of God was very strong. She lay on the floor for a long time. Marty occasionally moved her so that no one would step or fall on her.

Every time a new prayer line formed, Marty brought her up for prayer again. I must have prayed for her eight or nine times that night! Later, I mentioned her to Marty, and he shared that he had wanted her to get all the anointing she could. He'd never allowed her to go back to her seat. He'd just kept lifting her up and putting her back in line.

After I'd prayed for the sick, many people responded to the altar call for salvation. The little girl was one of them.

There were about thirty people at the altar when I suddenly sensed in the Holy Spirit that a wind was coming, almost like a twister. Though I sensed it coming closer, I didn't see anything moving in the tent. I knew it was going to hit this group while I was leading them in the salvation prayer. It was such a strong sense, that I was prompted to grab a baby one of the women was holding and handed the child to Marty.

Just then the Holy Spirit hit the group. People spun all over the floor, landing in every direction. As they fell under the power of God, they were praying in tongues. For a long time they just laid on the floor quivering. One of them was the little girl.

Little by little, people left. The power of God was so strong that there was no formal closing of the service. The little girl remained on the floor shaking, and I knelt down next to her.

After a few minutes she opened her eyes. I looked down into her tiny face and she asked me, "Where did He go?"

"What do you mean, honey?"

She said, "Jesus, Jesus! He was here with me the whole time and He said that I'm going to be all right."

About three months later, Marty and I were in California at a Rodney Howard-Brown convention. Several sponsoring pastors from our tent meeting in Washington state were there. They came and asked if we'd heard what happened to the little girl with leukemia. We said we hadn't heard anything about her.

"She was taken back to her doctors," they told us, "and they could not find a trace of leukemia in her! She's perfectly whole. Her hair has grown back and she's in school now!"

The "yoke" of leukemia was destroyed by the anointing!

Jesus is a wonderful God. He's a miracle-working God. Nothing is too hard for Him. No disease or pain or situation is too much for Him! He is the God who created the entire universe! And when we walk by faith, hearing His Holy Spirit, and obeying Him, we can walk in the miracle-working power of Jesus Christ and see souls saved, and people healed and delivered and set free.

Oh, that we would all hear and obey the Lord our God, knowing Jesus and the power of His crucifixion, and how much love was given to us on that Cross for you and me.

 **There is Power in the Blood of Jesus!**

Chapter 21

God's Perfect Timing

There are many kinds of miracles. Sometimes there are miracles we don't see coming, or ones we don't recognize at all until after they happen. Here is another story which shows how important it is to be sensitive to the Holy Spirit and obey Him right away.

The Lady at the Airport

I was once preaching in Pennsylvania, and the pastor and his wife brought me to the airport. They told me they'd stay until my plane arrived. I heard the Holy Spirit say, "Tell them to go away." So I said, "That's okay. I'll be fine."

"Oh no," they said. "We want to stay with you."

Not wanting to hurt their feelings, I just sat down and talked with them. But again I heard the Holy Spirit say, "Tell them to go. I've got something for you to do."

I told them I needed to go to the powder room and take care of some other things, but the pastor's wife insisted on going with me.

Pretty soon, the Holy Spirit simply said, "Why don't you just tell them?" So I told them, "I think God has me on an assignment right now and I need some time to myself."

As it turned out, because I delayed just those few minutes, I missed the timing of the Holy Spirit.

Soon after I'd said my goodbyes to them, my plane arrived and was ready for boarding. The passengers started to line up.

Suddenly I heard the Holy Spirit say, "See the lady there in line? I want you to go and hug her."

"You want me to do what?" I asked.

He said, "You just go and hug her."

Since the woman was now in line to board the plane, it was much more awkward to go and hug her than it would have been while she was sitting in the waiting area. Now I had to interrupt the whole line, including the stewardesses who were in charge.

I broke into the line, saying, "Excuse me. Excuse me," and stopped a whole group of people from boarding.

As I came face to face with the woman, the Holy Spirit said, "Just give her a great big hug." I was thinking, "Oh God, you don't just go hugging strange women at the airport! You don't just reach over and give a stranger a great big hug!" However I simply reached up and told her, "You need a hug." When it's the Holy Spirit, the best way to do it is to just jump into it!

As I hugged her, the Spirit of the Lord spoke through me saying, "Your husband has just asked you for a divorce. You have three children and you don't know how you're going to raise them. The Lord God Almighty says, "Your husband will not leave you. I am working mightily on your husband's behalf. He will turn around. He will serve Me. He will not divorce you. Be confident of this; God is working this out on your behalf."

All of this was coming out of my mouth and my mind was thinking, "I hope she's married. I hope she really does have three children."

She began crying and pushed me away. I was left there not knowing whether I was right or not, but she walked onto the plane saying, "Thank you Jesus! Praise you Jesus! Hallelujah! Hallelujah!"

Later, as we got off the plane, she came over to where I was seated and grabbed me by the hand. She said, "I don't know who you are, but my parents are Assembly of God pastors, and I was on my way home to tell them my husband just asked me for a divorce. Now I know it's all going to be fine! Thank you!"

God wants His children to hear accurately. When we ask Jesus to come into our hearts and be our LORD, it means that we are no longer our own. Our response to the voice of the Holy Spirit must be "Whatever you want me to do, however strange it may seem, I will be obedient."

As you are led by the Spirit, the devil will try to convince you that you're missing it. He tried to tell my mind, "When you try to hug this lady, she's going to call the police, or maybe punch you." Those kinds of thoughts may go through your head, too. But when it's God and you're being obedient to Him, things work out according to God's will for you.

After being tempted by the devil, Jesus left the wilderness and went to the synagogue in Nazareth. There he was handed the book of the prophet Isaiah.

> **....And when He had opened the book, He found the place where it was written: *"The Spirit of the LORD is upon Me, because He has anointed Me to preach the Gospel to the poor; He has sent Me to heal the brokenhearted, to proclaim liberty to the captives and recovery of sight to the blind, to set at liberty those who are oppressed; to proclaim the acceptable year of the LORD."***
>
> **Then He closed the book, and gave it back to the attendant and sat down. And the eyes of all who were in the synagogue were fixed on Him. And He began to say to them, "Today this Scripture is fulfilled in your hearing."** (Luke 4:17-21)

Jesus told those in the synagogue that the Scripture he had just read to them was "fulfilled in their hearing." And right after that, they tried to kill Him because of what He said.

> **So all those in the synagogue, when they heard these things, were filled with wrath, and rose up and thrust Him out of the city; and led**

> **Him to the brow of the hill on which their city was built, that they might throw Him down over the cliff. Then passing through the midst of them, He went His way.** (Luke 4:28-30)

As you see, though they wanted to kill Jesus, they couldn't, because it wasn't in God's plan. When you start to walk in the realm of the Spirit where you are led by the Spirit in everything, there are even Christians who will tell you that you have gone off the deep end. They will tell you you're "really getting out there." Yet if you love God, if you are madly in love with God, you will hear Him and you will obey!

Acts 10:38 tells us of how, **"God anointed Jesus of Nazareth with the Holy Spirit and with power, who went about doing good and healing all who were oppressed by the devil, for God was with Him."**

Let's look at how obedient Jesus was to the Holy Spirit. The Gospel of John, chapter 5:1-15, tells about a man who was healed at the pool of Bethesda. He had been an invalid for thirty-eight years. For many years he had been carried to the pool where **"a great multitude of sick people, blind, lame, paralyzed, [waited] for the moving of the water. For an angel went down at a certain time into the pool and stirred up the water; then whoever stepped in first, after the stirring of the water, was made well of whatever disease he had."** But this man was never able to get into the water fast enough.

Then one day Jesus went up to Jerusalem for a feast of the Jews and was walking by the pool where the man was.

> **When Jesus saw him lying there, and knew that he already had been in that condition a long time, He said to him, "Do you want to be made well?"**

The paralyzed man simply told Jesus his situation.

> **"Sir, I have no man to put me into the pool when the water is stirred up; but while I am coming, another steps down before me."**

So many of us might have given up going there every year. "I'm crippled. I'll never be able to get into the water. Why even bother going." Surely God saw this man's persistence.

Why did Jesus heal that particular man on that day at the pool of Bethesda? Because the Holy Spirit told Him, "Do you see the man over by the steps going into the pool? He has been coming here for many years, and he has never been able to get himself into the water. Go over to him."

Then **"Jesus said to him, 'Rise, take up your bed and walk.'"** Jesus obeyed the Holy Spirit.

In studying the life of Jesus, we learn that when we begin to walk in the Spirit, being led by the Holy Spirit, "religious" people are going to come against us. This literally happened to the paralyzed man whom Jesus healed on the Jewish Sabbath. It was unlawful to do any work on the Sabbath, including picking up the bed the man had been lying on.

The Pharisees asked him, **"Who is the Man who said to you, 'Take up your bed and walk'?"** But the man didn't know.

After the man found out it was Jesus, he went back and told the leaders. "It was Jesus who had made me well."

When the leaders confronted Jesus about what He had done, He clearly told them by what power and authority He performed miracles.

> **Then Jesus answered and said to them, "Most assuredly, I say to you, the Son can do nothing of Himself, but what He sees the Father do; for whatever He does, the Son also does in like manner."**
>
> (John 5:19)

Being able to walk on a higher level of relationship with the Father will require spending time recognizing and learning to hear the voice of the Holy Spirit.

It means you will have to be persistent, wanting more of the Holy Spirit, and less of yourself. Praying in the Holy Spirit will help you hear the Holy Spirit more clearly. The more you pray in the Holy Spirit, the more you will be able to hear God.

> **But you, beloved, building yourselves up on your most holy faith, praying in the Holy Spirit, keep yourselves in the love of God, looking for the mercy of our Lord Jesus Christ unto eternal life.** (Jude 20-21)

If you pray in the Spirit only a little bit, you may wind up questioning whether what you're hearing is from the Lord, the devil or yourself. It won't be clear to you. But when you pray fervently in the Spirit, you will know when it is God. You will know and recognize God's voice.

A married man can recognize the voice of his wife. Even if he were to be blindfolded and asked to pick out his wife's voice from the voices of several other women, he would be able to do it. He can recognize her voice because he has spent significant time with her.

The Holy Spirit is a gentle teacher. You can go to your teacher and say, "I don't understand this, Holy Spirit, and since you are my teacher, will you explain it to me a little better?"

When I began to step out in ministry, I did not know what to do. But I would constantly say, "Holy Spirit, you are the teacher, and I need help! I don't know quite how to hear you yet. I get confused sometimes, but I know you will help me." It is the Holy Spirit Himself who will help you start to recognize and hear His voice.

Pray every day: Holy Spirit help me and teach me.

Chapter 22

God Will Make a Way

As you move closer to God and are able to recognize His voice more clearly, He will be able to use you in deeper ways. You will be able to move in the supernatural. God Himself will draw people to you. Miracles will follow as you speak His Word under the leading of the Holy Spirit.

While doing a tent revival meeting at Foursquare Church in Hollister, California several years ago, we prayed for supernatural encounters to happen, so that people would be drawn to the tent to hear about Jesus.

God answered and people began to be drawn in. They had no idea why they were led to come there. Then God began to draw people to us when we were doing things outside the tent area.

One day we were taken to a Mexican restaurant to celebrate Marty's birthday. As the waitress handed us menus, we suddenly heard someone crying. Though the restaurant was full of people all four of us at the table heard it. We looked up and saw the waitress standing there with her pad in hand, waiting to take our orders. Tears were streaming down her face.

"What's the matter, honey," I asked.

She said, "You guys are the ones doing the tent meeting, right? I want to get right with God. I want to give my heart to Jesus!"

What a joy it was for us to answer her heart's cry and lead her to the Lord.

Everywhere we went it was like that. In front of stores and on city sidewalks people would ask us to pray for them. Some of them even fell under the power of God. It was really incredible how God drew people to the tent.

Released from Jail

After the services the next night, we went to another restaurant. The waitress brought water to our table, and the Holy Spirit said to me, "She is supposed to be at the tent; you need to get her to the tent."

So I told her, "Honey, you need to come to the tent."

She said, "Oh, you mean the big red and white tent up the street?"

I said, "Yeah."

She replied, "I can't go, I'm in jail."

I said, "You don't look like you're in jail."

It turned out she was on a work release program which allowed her to work the night shift, starting at 10:00 p.m. until morning. She said she couldn't go to the tent meeting; but the Holy Spirit said, "Yes, she can."

When she came back to our table, I told her "You can go." Then I told her a story about another woman

I knew who had been in jail.

We had a Holy Ghost Explosion where we lived. A woman in jail heard one of my testimony tapes while she was in a halfway house. She saw our advertisement for a two-day Signs and Wonders Explosion while watching T.V. in the city jail. She said to herself, "Lord, I really want to go to that meeting, but I still have six more weeks of jail time. If there's any way, I want to go to the meeting and give my heart to you, Jesus."

The day of the meetings came, and she was still sitting in her jail cell. At 6:30 p.m. the jailer came to her cell and told her, "You're out of here girl. Get your stuff."

She said, "But I have six more weeks."

The jailer said, "No you don't. I don't know why, but you better get out while you can. I don't know if it's a mix up with the paperwork or what, but they told me to let you out. Get your stuff!"

She left the jail, and walked to the meeting, arriving ten minutes late.

That night she was saved and filled with the Holy Spirit.The following evening, she came again, and helped lead some teens to Christ.

"You see," I told our waitress, "God got that woman out of jail when she had six more weeks to go. If he wants you at the tent meeting, they will have to let you out early. We can pray right now for that to happen."

We all joined hands and prayed over the situation. Our friend Judy said she would call the jail to see if they would let her out.

The next day, while I was in prayer seeking the Lord for the day's message and praying for the services, I had a vision. I saw the waitress walking into the tent meeting. When she walked up to me, I simply said to her "You want to receive Jesus, don't you?" And she accepted Jesus just like that.

That night we were at the tent and about to close the service. We had already prayed for the sick and for people to come to Jesus and be filled with the Holy Spirit. We had an altar call and were ready to give the final prayer.

Suddenly my husband motioned to me not to finish yet. I looked towards the back entrance, and there was the waitress. She had been let out of jail a half hour early, with permission to go to the tent on her way to work. I had Marty bring her up front.

She walked right up to me. When I looked into her eyes I got a flashback of the vision I'd had that morning.

I said to her, "You want to receive Jesus, don't you?" And she said, "Yes."

She wasn't there for the preaching; she was there to receive Jesus.

What was so awesome was when I told her to say, "Dear Jesus, come into my heart...." That was as far as she got. She was suddenly going down under the power of the Holy Spirit. Marty tried to catch her, but the presence of the Lord was so strong that he collapsed too. Even someone who tried to catch her from the other side fell out. There she was. She was even beginning to speak in tongues!

We thought the meeting was over, when suddenly a wave of the Spirit came into the tent. A whole section of people started jumping out of their seats. Elderly women were dancing, singing and shouting "Hallelujah! Praise God!" The Holy Spirit literally moved in a powerful and dramatic way. All kinds of miraculous things happened. Lives were changed forever.

It was all so wonderful because we knew what happened was all God!

Chapter 23

We Can Do the Will of the Father

As you've been reading this book, you've been seeing that you too can hear God, and do His will. You can walk in the supernatural realm as Jesus did, totally under the leading of the Holy Spirit. Jesus told us He only did what the Father showed Him to do. That word applies to us today. The Spirit of God showed me that he wants us to live as Jesus did.

> **"I can of Myself do nothing. As I hear, I judge; and my judgment is righteous, because I do not seek My own will but the will of the Father who sent Me."** (John 5:30)

That's how we are to live daily, saying, "Not my will God, but Your will." Each day we should be asking Him, "Holy Spirit, what do You want me to do? Where do you want me to go? What do you want me to say." The Holy Spirit will lead us.

> **"Do you not believe that I am in the Father, and the Father in Me? The words that I speak to you I do not speak on My own authority; but the Father who dwells in Me does the works.**

Believe Me that I am in the Father and the Father in Me, or else believe Me for the sake of the works themselves." (John 14:10-11)

In this passage, Jesus is telling His disciples that if they don't want to take His word that He does the works through the Father, then they should believe because of what they see happening. This touches upon the fact that we who are in Christ should be walking in the power of God. When the world sees what God does in and through us, they will experience the presence of God and be drawn to Jesus.

"Most assuredly, I say to you, he who believes in me, the works that I do he will do also; and greater works than these he will do, because I go to My Father. And whatever you ask in My name, that I will do, that the Father may be glorified in the Son." (John 14:12-13)

The Father is glorified in people being saved, healed and delivered!

"If you ask anything in My name, I will do it. If you love Me, keep My commandments. And I will pray the Father, and He will give you another Helper, that He may abide with you forever...." (John 14:14-16)

How long will the Helper abide with us? Forever! The Holy Spirit is our Helper.

> **"But the Helper, the Holy Spirit, whom the Father will send in My name, He will teach you all things, and bring to your remembrance all things that I said to you. Peace I leave with you, My peace I give to you; not as the world gives do I give to you. Let not your heart be troubled, neither let it be afraid.** (John 14:26-27)

And today the Lord is saying to you, "Do not be afraid to step out into the things of God; do not be afraid to step out into the things of the Spirit."

The End Time revival that is going to sweep through the world is going to be done by an outpouring of the Holy Spirit. For this reason you must prepare your heart. When we, as God's people, become so saturated with the Holy Spirit, we will say, "None of me; Lord, all of You." There will be a hunger in you to be used of God.

Ten O'Clock Meeting

One time I ministered in a church in Arizona, where I'd never met the pastor. Somehow I still didn't get an opportunity to meet the pastor and his wife after I'd preached the morning service. I just went back to my hotel. While I was in my room praying, the Holy Spirit told me to go down to the coffee shop and ask them what time they closed. I did, and they told me10:00 p.m.

I asked the hostess, "If I came in at 9:45 would you wait on me?" She said, "Yes, but we close at ten."

Suddenly the Holy Spirit told me to ask her, "If I came in at 9:50, would you wait on me?"

Again she said yes, but they closed at ten. The Holy Spirit said to ask, "If I came in at 9:55, would you wait on me?"

She repeated the same answer, yes, but they closed at ten.

Then the Holy Spirit had me ask her, "If I came in at one minute to ten, would you wait on me?"

She said, "Yes, but we close at ten." I thanked the hostess and went back to my room. I must admit to thinking, "I wonder why the Lord had me do all that!"

Later that night I was preaching the evening service at the church. I still hadn't had a chance to talk with the pastor. Following the service, I was at my book table when suddenly the Holy Spirit said, "You need to go to the hotel coffee shop, and you need to go right now!"

I thought, "But it's ten minutes to ten!" The Lord said, "You have to take the pastor and his wife with you."

The pastor was counseling someone, and didn't know me very well. But I walked over and said, "Excuse me, pastor, I hate to interrupt when you're counseling, but do you know the coffee shop at the hotel where I'm staying? We have to go there, right now!"

The pastor looked at me and said, "Well right now, I'm busy." I said, "Okay."

But the Lord said, "Look, it's seven minutes to ten! They have to be at the coffee shop. Get them and go there now!"

I walked over to the pastor again and said, "Pastor, we really have to go. It's seven minutes to ten and we have to be at the coffee shop."

"I don't like that coffee shop," he told me. "There's another one that's open until eleven."

I told the Holy Spirit I didn't know what to do. He said, "Just get them."

I looked at my watch; it was now five minutes to ten! I was frantic. How could I get them to the coffee shop by one minute to ten! I don't know how it happened, but finally we all hurried out and got in the car.

The pastor, his wife and I walked into the coffee shop at one minute to ten. We didn't have a clue about why we were there. I told the hostess we'd like a table for three. She looked at the clock and said, "It's one minute to ten."

I said, "Yes, but you told me earlier today that if I got here by one minute to ten you would wait on me."

She said, "Well the grill's closed."

I said, "We won't eat, just let us in. We'll have something to drink."

She said, "We're just getting ready to pour everything out."

I said, "We'll just have water." She agreed, and sat us at a table. She threw down some menus and sent the waitress over.

The waitress came with three glasses of water. When I looked at her, I heard the Holy Spirit say, "Ask her if she wants to get born again."

Now that was something! I never use that phrase, because most people don't understand what it means. When I teach about witnessing I steer away from the phrase "getting born again" because most people are still trying to figure out how they got born the first time in the natural, never mind about a second time in the spirit!

Still the Holy Spirit directed me to ask this woman if she wanted to be born again. So being obedient to the voice of the Spirit, I asked her.

She exclaimed, "Oh! You've got to be kidding! This is wonderful! Did you ask me if I wanted to get born again?"

She was all excited and reached into her pocket. She said, "Look at this! See this. It's a letter from my friend. She used to be a drug addict, but I don't understand what happened to her. She went to Los Angeles and she's been writing me letters for two months. Something has changed. When I talk to her on the phone, all she talks about is Jesus! She's been totally changed, I mean radically!"

"But look at this letter. I've been carrying it with me for a week. You see? I have it highlighted here.

She says right here that I have to find somebody who knows how to get me born again."

Then she said, "I'm ready! I'm ready! What do I have to do?"

It was so neat, because there was no one in the coffee shop except us. She prayed and invited Jesus into her heart, saying, "Thank you Jesus! I'm born again! Hallelujah! I'm born again now!"

I told her, **"If any man be in Christ, he is a new creation."** (2Corinthians 5:17.) And I shared other scriptures with her.

Then she said, "There's only one other thing in the letter from my friend. Let me read it to you. It's right here: 'After you find somebody and get born again, find a good pastor and a pastor's wife.'"

"Do you know where I can find a good pastor and pastor's wife?"

"Yes," I said, "these people right here."

The Holy Spirit made sure everything that waitress needed was right there. She had been crying out to God. She didn't know how, but God answered her cry!

When we learn to hear and obey the voice of the Holy Spirit, He will orchestrate our footsteps to answer everyone's heart cry. There are people crying out all over the world saying,

"Oh God, my marriage is falling apart."

"My children are on drugs, God."

"Oh God, my finances are a wreck!"

"Oh God, if you really are real, can you hear my heart cry?"

God hears the heart cry of the neighbor down the street, and the person working at the convenience store, and the person at the gas station. God will answer their cries by using the Christian who is willing to be obedient. God will use the Christian who will hear and not question, the one willing to do what the Father says.

God wants all of us to be that Christian — the one who will say, "Yes" to God, no matter what He asks us to do.

Yes, YOU can hear GOD too! Open your heart to God. Simply say: "Here am I, God. Use me, send me, Holy Spirit lead me."

Beloved, as you have read this book you have read many stories about people whose lives have been changed forever. God loves people and He sent His Son Jesus so they can have eternal life.

God loves you very much and wants you in His Kingdom.

For God so loved the world that He gave His only begotten Son, that whoever believes in Him should not perish but have eternal life. (John 3:16)

God said, "WHOEVER!" That means You! You can come to Jesus Right Now. God wants you in Heaven and to have eternal life. Here is what God says:

...if you confess with your mouth the Lord Jesus and believe in your heart that God has raised Him from the dead, you will be saved.

For with the heart one believes unto righteousness, and with the mouth confession is made unto salvation.

(Romans 10:9-10)

Just believe and receive the free gift of eternal life.

Pray this prayer now!

Father in Heaven, I know I am a sinner.
I am sorry for my sins.
I believe that Jesus died on the cross for me,
And that He rose again and ascended into Heaven.
I love you Jesus.
I invite you, Jesus, into my heart
To be my personal Savior.
I will love you, obey you, and serve you
For all of my life.
Thank you Jesus for saving my soul.
Amen.

About Channel of Love Ministries

Evangelist Joan Pearce was radically saved in 1977, and shortly afterwards moved to Washington State. There she was greatly inspired and discipled by the daughter and son-in-law of late Evangelist John G. Lake. God asked Joan to step out and do in-home Bible Studies, even though she couldn't read.

Joan recognized God's hand was on her, and that He was calling her into ministry. Her heart cry is for souls and to fulfill Luke 4:18-19, "to preach the gospel to the poor," heal the brokenhearted, and bring healing and freedom to the hurting and oppressed — "to proclaim the acceptable year of the Lord."

Today Joan continues in full-time ministry, traveling across the United States and overseas. Channel of Love Ministries is doing "God is Taking the City" campaigns, where Joan and her husband Marty are seeing churches come together in unity to evangelize their cities. Joan also does revivals, church meetings, and city-wide crusades where thousands come to Jesus. Part of her ministry is to teach practical evangelism classes and to conduct Holy Spirit Miracle Services where there are many notable and creative miracles. She and Marty have a heart to feed and clothe the needy and have ministered to the poor throughout the world.

Joan is on TV across the United States. To learn more about Channel of Love's resource materials and ongoing ministry, check the website at www.joanpearce.org.

Channel of Love Ministries Intl.

Helping you to grow spiritually and share your faith more effectively!

Yes, YOU can hear GOD too!

Order No. 0007-B

Price $15.00

Every believer has the right to hear from Heaven. This down to earth book will challenge **you** to hear from God!

Let's Go Fishing!

Order No. 0042-B

Price $15.00

Are you wondering? "What's God's purpose and plan for my life?" "How do I: Draw my loved ones and others to the Lord.... Answer their questions.... Help my church or group reach out to the lost and needy?" This book answers your questions.

Now's the Time Bible Studies

Order No. 0043-B

Price $10.00

Here are precious keys for unlocking and releasing God-given provision, power and authority into your life, and experiencing the precious love of Jesus. You'll grow spiritually -- and be able to share what you've learned with others.

The Empty Spot

Order No. 0045-B

Price per pkg. of 10 $12.00

An excellent booklet for getting people saved and for discipling those who have recently received Jesus. This book has led thousands to Jesus. It's a great witnessing tool!

BOOK ORDER FORM

You can also order on our website: **www.joanpearce.org**

Special orders or **quantity orders**: contact us at our website or by phone.

Cat. #	Description	Price	Qty	Sub-Total
0007-B	**Yes, You Can Hear GOD, too!**	**$15.00**		
0042-B	**Let's Go Fishing!**	**$15.00**		
0043-B	**Now's the Time Bible Studies**	**$10.00**		
0045-B	**Empty Spot - Pkg. of 10**	**$12.00**		

Please allow 2-3 weeks for delivery	**Sub-Total**	
Mail Order Form and payment to: **Channel of Love Ministries, Intl.** **PO Box 458** **Red Bluff, CA 96080** **877-852-6194 (office)**	**S/H** Add 30% of Sub-Total	
	Total	

❑ **Payment enclosed** ❑ **MasterCard** ❑ **VISA**

Card # ______________________ **Exp.** ____________

Phone # __________ **Signature** ______________________
(Req.)

Name ____

Address ______________________________________

____

City ____________________________ **State** __________

ZIP ______________ **EMail** ________________________